Two White Feathers and a Handful of Rocks

a woman's journey through the feminine ch'amas of South and Central America

Jenny Chapman

Copyright

The moral right of Jenny Chapman to be identified as the author of this work has been asserted by her in accordance with the Copyright, Designs and Patents Act of 1988.

All events in this story happened but, as with Stephen Hawking's concept of time, they did not necessarily happen in the order written.

All rights reserved. No part of this publication may be reproduced, stored in retrieval systems, or transmitted in any form or by any means, electronic, mechanical, photocopying, recording or otherwise without prior permission by the copyright owner.

Every effort has been made to trace or contact all copyright holders. The publisher will be pleased to make good any omissions or rectify any mistakes brought to their attention at the earliest opportunity.

All photographs within this book were taken by Jenny Chapman except for page 51 (Edgar our taxi driver), page 73 (Apu Runa), page 127 (Jenny Lynne Sessions - Jen-ix) and page 128 (Maria Moonstar and Jeff) who retain copyright on all these images.

ISBN 978-0-9956188-0-0

Author's note

This book is a fictionalised account based on real events. It is not intended to accurately document any person or place. To write this book I relied on interview transcripts, my personal journals, research and my own memory of events both during the trip and in my lifetime. In the book, I have changed the names of some but not all of the individuals and modified some details to preserve anonymity. Some characters are composites of different people. Some people or events have been omitted but only when the omission had little impact on the substance of the story.

I am not an expert in Mesoamerican, including Andean and Mayan, shamanic practices or prophesies and have made every attempt to check the information contained in this book with indigenous people who are qualified to talk about these areas.

Contents

Map		5
Foreword		6 - 7
The Lead Up		8 - 17
Ch'ama One	The Story	18 - 31
Ch'ama Two	Breakthrough	32 - 45
Ch'ama Three	Embodiment	46 - 59
Ch'ama Four	A Bridge	60 - 73
Ch'ama Five	Getting Help	74 - 85
Ch'ama Six	Becoming Whole	86 - 97
Ch'ama Seven	Connecting to Self	98 - 111
Postscript		112 - 117
A note on *ch'amas* and *chakras*		118 - 120
A note on condors		121
A note on shamanic healing		122 - 125
Endnotes		126 - 129

For dad and his help with our vision of a healing centre

1. Buenos Aires
2. Uspallata
3. Parque Provincial Aconcagua
4. Santiago & Valparaíso
5. La Serena
6. Puno
7. Qosqo
8. Lima
9. Churin
10. Huaraz
11. Chavin de Huantar
12. Yungay
13. Trujillo
14. Bogotá
15. Cartagena
16. San Agustín
17. Mocoa
18. Cancún
19. Mérida
20. Piste
21. Tulum
22. Ciudad de México
23. Puebla
24. Teotihuacán
25. Tula
26. Popocatépetl

Above: Feminine Ch'ama Route

Foreword

Early on in our feminine *ch'ama* pilgrimage Apu Runa said to me, 'Jenny, I have taken your idea and I want to open a spiritual healing centre.' 'That's good,' I replied, 'but you should know the idea came from Maria Moonstar who is particularly keen to assist disempowered Peruvian women and young people who often live in conditions of poverty and are vulnerable to abuse, particularly sexual abuse.' I also had those suffering from disability, illness and injuries in mind, since my work for thirty years had involved them. I wanted to make the centre accessible to everyone.

Apu's offer to build the centre was not discussed again until Colombia, when he talked of wanting to buy land on his return to Peru. I repeated my pledge to donate profits from this book to help, but he said, 'That might take years. We need the spiritual centre now.'

I trusted Apu's motives and his ability to help people, as he is a healer and shaman. He trained with his master, Don Petro Huaman Quispe for 10 years, and when he passed away in 1999, Apu continued to work and study alone. Once, whilst travelling together in a motor taxi, he let down his guard and talked of inviting a man dying from AIDS to live with him. At other times, he assisted with the love-life of a dwarf and healed a man considered mad because he saw mermaids. He spoke of his commitment to community work and, under pressure from me, said that when the community struggled to help someone they then turned to him, and that he often healed people in need for free. This was reinforced by his actions on our pilgrimage during which he went out of his way to help and heal people and once tried to share a 100 sol payment with me.

Late in 2015, Apu purchased land in the village of Ichu-fondo, about 14 kilometres south of Puno. He would build a spiritual centre step-by-step on the shores of Lake Titicaca, which is considered the sexual *ch'ama* of the world. The site is guarded by the sacred waters of the lake and a huge stone phallus high in the hills. In the distance can be seen the ancient Piramide de Inca Tunuhuiri where he eventually plans to hold ceremonies.

Apu is keen for spiritual tourists to learn the lessons of the *ch'amas* and lead a shamanic way of life. This is a life anchored in the 'here and now' and cleansed of negative thoughts and environments. Here the path is bright. Action and good example are as important as humour and play. Apu would like us to feel the energies of *Pachamama* in our bodies and be guided by the intelligence of the heart; to vibrate harmoniously and have no fears or expectations in our daily experiences. It can be a challenging road, particularly for people from the Western world.

In January 2016, Don José Morales, a journalist friend of Apu, visited the walled site with us. We were greeted by Illapa, Apu's yellow dog, named after his beloved master Don Pedro Huamán Quispe whose name meant 'lightning bolt'. On entering through the gate we walked across the dirt to Apu's small, incomplete house. On the ground floor, the first room was destined to be his clinic and altar. In my mind's eye I saw a queue of people waiting for healings, just like the ones patiently waiting to receive their treatments when he first visited his master's house in Ollantaytambo.

Standing on the roof of Apu's half-completed house we looked down on a circular ceremonial construction about waist high, and another smaller circular building destined for cleansing work using hot steam. Around the circular buildings medicinal herb gardens would be planted. Opposite his house a small hotel with comfortable rooms was planned. Apu explained how the far area before the round buildings was for growing vegetables and fruit trees. He hoped the spiritual healing centre would be self-sufficient and offer a healthy diet to locals, spiritual tourists and other visitors.

We were entranced. In time, Don José added the idea of beautiful perfumed flowers growing up the stark block walls to make the small plot a paradise. In town, Apu and I purchased some herbs, cleansing plants and a rose to help establish this new vision.

The Lead Up

Shamans, witches, wizards and magicians are powerful men and women. So what could have possessed me, a woman of fifty-four years, to travel alone with one through South and Central America for seven weeks? I could only trust he would be waiting for me in the mountains of Argentina, that we might communicate by way of Spanglish and that my body would manage the hardship and back-break of gruelling bus travel. Just one night's accommodation was pre-booked for the whole trip and I hadn't considered where we might sleep should money run short. More importantly, I failed to realise the trip would involve more than just the two of us; that this shaman had a message to deliver and together he intended that we should help activate the feminine *ch'amas* for ourselves and others.

I loved Apu's energy from the start. He was compassionate, kind and almost empty, invisible; but he could be blunt, verging on outright rude at times. In other words, he was my kind of person, telling it like it is. Or, as the Australians say, he called a spade a spade. 'I will do whatever is necessary to get you to shift, learn and move on in life,' he told me on the road and he was true to his word. An Andean priest, Apu's first principle is to serve humanity – to be a channel for the Goddess *Pachamama* (Mother Earth) and deliver healings. With twenty-five years of shamanic training and practice, and the ability to alter a person's DNA or energy fields and restructure and realign experiences to manifest a different reality,[1] he was not a man to be trifled with.

There was a natural timing and synchronicity to my introduction to Apu, one of the most important shamans in the Americas to have studied the *ch'amas*. I possessed the adequate funds and was at a point in my life where I was happy to embark on a new life chapter. The trip wasn't conceived as an adventure, but that's what it proved to be. In many ways it just happened. There was a natural flow, with travel and logistics falling into place.

Six months before the pilgrimage itself, in Puno, a bean reading by Apu with black seeds known as *huayruros*, predicted significant change for me. This was a strange affair in which your future is read according to how the small red and black beans fall. Apu said, 'You need to learn to trust in matters of the heart and open the door to opportunity. Change the way you earn money, take care of your body and put yourself first so you have the energy to work with other people and remove doubt from your spiritual path.' He predicted that I would teach people through my writing, work with children and educate them in spiritual ways. 'You are a white witch! The spiritual path is magical if you open your heart and trust.' More than once, with a mix of frustration and consternation on his face, he said, 'Remember your flight with the Condor.'

Arriving in Buenos Aires I was unsure of our plan and how it would come together. Apu's small daily rate, calculated to be affordable, was already in his bank account and he seemed true to his word. But at the back of my mind I wondered whether this would be a no-show, or whether we would struggle to connect and work together over the weeks ahead. Whilst Apu was used to working with spiritual tourists, travelling long distances on public transport and going with the flow, I possessed an obsession with work that had at times become problematic, making me incapable of heart-based thinking. I feared I might not prove the easiest of travel companions.

It is fair to say I had been busy unravelling my work persona over the previous couple of years. My job involved vulnerable people (people returning to work after illness or injury) and I needed to resolve my own issues in an effort to become more effective. Aware that out reflects in – and that my out wasn't looking too clever in 2012 – I enrolled at an all-woman shamanism school in Star House, Dorset. It was a big step. Before I met Eliana, the owner and main trainer, I picked up Caitlin Mathew's book *Singing the Soul Back Home* and remember thinking it was not only a big step, but a step too far. The notion of talking to land spirits and 'calling in' energies didn't sit comfortably with me. Even my rural English farm childhood – hours on horseback meandering through the country lanes, connecting with the land, trees and animals – didn't allay my fears.

Little did I anticipate the powerful impact and release of those years under Eliana's tutelage. My year-group learned to address inappropriate female and male energies and access the upper and lower worlds through trance ('journeying'). Each of us re-found our inner child. My favourite exercise at the women's training school involved blindfolds, the kind of noises used to call a dog or horse, and telepathy.[2] Later in my training I helped with the new first year students. I 'held space' – that is, balanced the energies in the room so as to maintain calm – and delivered Munai Ki rites[3] in ceremonial costume. Our work was mostly experiential, often fun and sometimes shocking. Screams and shouts echoed through the building, making the hairs on my neck stand up. Each training weekend, come Sunday evening I was spent. I quietly processed my experiences for days afterwards.

Before setting off on the *ch'ama* pilgrimage I was coming to the end of what might be called a 'mid-life career crisis.' Yes, I was slightly burned out with responsibility - managing a business twenty-four-seven and bearing the emotional toll of listening to client stories - but it was more than that. I felt unclean and as if old issues were impacting on my work. I worried about projecting my rubbish onto my clients and was no longer a good Rehabilitation Counsellor. My desire to create positive change had dried up. The problem was how to cleanse my system and rekindle a flame in my heart and passion for my work.

It was not the first time. As a 21-year-old fresh out of University, it took a precognisant dream to lead me to the end of a significant romance and to undertake a nine-month sailing trip which restored my love of life. In my late 30's, having changed house, partner and job, I made a three week train journey back from Australia to the UK. The trip across China, Mongolia, Russia and Europe was effortless and seemed almost pre-destined. These trips heralded a change of chapter, a major transition in my life, and I wondered if this one might prove the same.

Trained at Star House, most years Maria Moonstar recruited an excited group of women to tour the Americas. Word had it, nobody ever returned the same. Lives were changed, and mine would be too. Our group travelled with a number of shamans including Don Basilio, an Andean priest whose open smile lit up his face. Following a long day of ceremony at the dizzying heights of Machu Picchu, he gave us the *Hatun Karpay* rite[4] at Moray, along with cocoa leaf readings.

Before the trip to the Americas, I dreamt of a man so vividly that when I awoke I fully expected him to be beside my bed. Dressed in the colourful, beaded hat replete with woollen pompoms traditionally worn by Andean priests, now Don Basilio said to me: 'Mother Earth is helping you. The man who came to you in a dream was an Apu (the spirit of a person who lives in sacred terrain such as a mountain). Try *Ayahuasca*. You will meet a high priest who will help you on the route to Puno.' Finally, he said, 'Do you know your spiritual name? It is *'Hatun Sonqo'*. This means big heart or spirit.'

His prediction was reinforced in the ancient market town of Pizac, about twenty miles from Qosqo, by Joanna, a psychic: 'You have a big, childlike spirit,' she told me. 'Open your heart and see the signs.' She talked of relations, 'for a few days, a month, a trip together,' with a man I would meet. 'A very special person with a strong temperament. A shaman perhaps. A bit of a clown, you will know him since he makes this peculiar face.' And with that she twisted her eyebrows up and started waggling them.

Like me, my roommate Julia had also sailed the oceans and lived in Australia for a number of years. We met on a retreat in Italy. There were other women on the trip with whom I had trained and worked at Star House – Karry, Ros, Berni, Rosemary and Mary – and some fascinating newcomers. One of these, Mo, used her nose to smell out solutions and answer spiritual questions. Imagine someone's nose twitching every time you told the truth! Mo spent long hours on the bus tapping out[5] the reason for my fear of heights, and recalibrating my being. For years, like my father and several of my siblings, I had been frightened of heights because of my desire to jump. As a fourteen-year-old I had wanted to leap from the Eiffel Tower, and more recently felt the same at the 'Gherkin' in London. Mo said in a previous life I had had no option but to jump, no doubt to my death. Not only that, I had led others to their demise. So it was no wonder I was scared.

On the tour, we travelled the well-worn routes of the sacred sites with shamans, psychics and healers and benefited from the insight of anthropologists, biologists and plant experts. Once the group had gone home, Maria Moonstar took me to the high plateaux, jungle and Peruvian islands. We visited the sacred mountain of Ausengate, were introduced to medicinal jungle plants in Puerto Maldernado and watched men knitting in Taquile. I touched the energy fields and lines at Nasca and watched the condors fly at Colca Canyon. Along the way I camped high up in the fresh snowfall, stayed in a luxury hotel which appeared to float on the vastness of Lake Titicaca, sampled backstreet market food and ceviche and met simple, clean-living Andean people and fast-thinking, money-rich Westerners. I joined in wild folk-dancing and rode on the most comfortable of horses. Maria Moonstar would also introduce me to Apu.

Returning from the Islands of the Sun and Moon in Bolivia, as the tour bus passed Spirit Valley I was entranced, drawn to the land in some way. I later asked Maria Moonstar to recommend a guide in the Puno area, south of Qosqo. At the close of the three-week tour, she led me to Apu's relatives in their Qosqo shop. Walking away from the main square where the cathedral overlooks the women in national costume selling photographs of themselves with their llamas, we hustled through the busy back streets to ask if he was in the country. 'Yes, he's in Puno,' a woman replied pleasantly. 'I'm sure he would love to hear from you.'

Some weeks later, having organised a visit – by telephone – to the Aramu Muru doorway, Apu collected me from my *pension* at the appointed hour. He was pleased Maria Moonstar had recommended him to work with me. 'That's good,' he said. In the car his warm brown eyes gazed at me as he told me about the feminine *ch'amas*. He spoke passionately about a majestic mountain in Argentina, the pure energies of Amantani islanders and Qosqo – his birthplace, where once Sapa Incas could heal with one touch. Chavin, the heart *ch'ama*, sounded to me like the Peruvian equivalent of my local town Glastonbury in the UK. 'How do you spell Aconcagua?' I asked.

He paused to see if I was following his broken English. Putumayo in Colombia is the throat *ch'ama*, Chichen Itza in the Yucatan represents the third eye and Teotihuacan in Mexico represents the crown. 'I don't know these particular three places as I have never been there,' he admitted. He explained the *ch'amas* (representing the 7 *chakras*, see note on page 118) lay in the feminine part of *Pachamama*. The mountain range of the Andes represented their backbone whilst the *chakras* of the Western or Oriental

Above: Illustration of the Ch'amas

Above: The Condor's Nest

traditions are masculine and their vertebral column lies in the Himalayan Mountain range.

Apu gazed out of the car window then turned to me and said dramatically, 'the Himalayas used to dominate the energy of the planet but they are now coming to rest, while in the Andes the feminine part of the Earth is stirring.'

I had a lot to take in. After an hour we arrived at a huge snake-like boulder and Apu took strange-looking shamanic tools from his brightly coloured bag and laid them on a rock. 'I ask permission to enter these sacred lands,' he said. Then we moved into the Valley of the Spirits, where I had seen intriguing stone figures from the bus. Over an hour-and-a-half hike, Apu told stories and gave vivid interpretations of family groups and caterpillars. Then he declared we had arrived at the condor's nest and asked if I wanted to go flying. That is, did I want to partake in an Andean initiation?

I felt both scared and excited. What could the initiation possibly involve and how do you learn to fly, particularly from a nest so high and over such a vast landscape? Pointing at a rock he told me to prepare myself for the ceremony of the Flight of the Condor. As I lay in the warm sunshine, Mo's tapping came to me. After half an hour, Apu beckoned me over. 'Close your eyes, now fly.' On his instruction my eyes opened, then a strange, guttural sound came from deep within my body and leaving my mouth in a long sigh. First I needed the help of Apu's kind words and a demonstration, then I flew. After flying, Apu bent down and placed two small, white feathers in my hand. 'These are for you,' he said. Then we continued walking towards the Aramu Muru doorway.

Flower and fruit offerings in our hands perfumed the way. On arrival, a ceremony with singing bowls, offerings of coca and sprinklings of Florida and Kananga water[6] allowed Apu to contact the local spirit guards. I stood by his side, watching intently. Legend has it that during the wedding of two star-crossed lovers, the young groom went to receive his bride from the opposite village. While the wedding party was dancing past the doorway, one of the musicians discreetly slipped behind some

Above: Aramu Muru doorway

This Page: Burial Chamber

rocks to answer a call of nature. As the dancing continued, the solid rock doorway opened to reveal a parallel world which shone beautifully. It was an etheric city.[7] The musician watched helplessly as it re-closed before his eyes, leaving him behind, like the lame boy from Hamelin, to tell the tale.

Permission granted, and the doorway open, Apu told me to make contact with the door and feel the wonderful energies. A gentle push and I tentatively approached the massive carved doorways with my flower offering. In the right-hand doorway, I knelt with my hands spread out against the cold stone sides, and after a few minutes I went to the left, before finally approaching the central portal. I briefly felt myself leave my body and returned to Apu refreshed and reinvigorated. Later, Apu described the mysterious people he saw whilst I was there. 'Two teachers, dressed in white. They didn't walk but rather seemed to float.'

Above: Apu entering the tomb

> *She will be your guide in the physical world and you will guide her towards an awakening and remembrance of the spiritual path begun in other lives.*

Ours was a reciprocal meeting, he said.

> *Do not doubt whether to accept this proposal. The masters have planned it for both of you and you will encounter the new time together.*

Above: Apu preparing my 'love' despacho

Apu said he was distracted by what they said to him, and the word *ayni* (reciprocity) resounded in his mind. 'Do you know what *ayni* means, Jenny?' he asked.

In the car back we talked a little more. I was happy but tired. As the taxi tyres vibrated on the long road I gently slipped away. My body shifted into that of a massive bird, and wings sprouted where my arms once were. It seemed as if I might be one of those small planes that took aerial photographs of your house in the '70's. I flew over a stony valley, covering an immense distance easily. Then I glided on a thermal, high up into the deep blue sky. My piercing eyesight surveyed the land below. Hungry for my dinner, I searched for the dead.

On our return to Puno we visited the temple of fertility in Chucuito, with its multiple stones shaped like mushrooms. These phallic monuments are used by farmers in ceremonies to thank Mother Earth. Sat on top, Apu asked about my wishes and dreams. 'What about love, Jenny?' At the hotel we parted.

Over the following days Apu worked a little more with me. Quite windswept, we went up into the mountains for our 'ceremony of the here and now.' Apu whistled to the eagles as we walked. At the summit he declared we would work in an old tomb and crawled under a low stone doorway beckoning me to follow. On our last day together he suggested a love ceremony in the ceremonial space high above the city of Puno. First, we purchased the ceremonial offerings and some dung for a bonfire. Under a white cross at the top of a high mountain called Azoguini, he entered another dimension and reconfigured my future. Back on solid ground I felt as if my world had shifted.

Three months later, back in the UK, I wrote an email to Apu proposing he guide me on a trip to the seven *ch'amas* of *Pachamama* of which he had spoken. He told me of his teacher, Don Pedro Huaman Quispe. It was due to him that he could name the *ch'amas* and narrate stories about them. Over the last ten years he had studied and made enquiries with old masters who confirmed the stories. 'In the memory of the old oral tradition of the Andean priests, these energetic points are known to exist. But I have not physically visited them before, and am not qualified to guide you,' he said. Then he recalled the voices in the doorway which indicated we should guide each other, and so agreed to make the trip; dates were proposed and the journey begun.

By September, I had put the necessary building blocks in place.

Apu and I first met on the shores of Lake Titicaca, Peru on 28th April 2014. Our next meeting would be at a bus station in Mendoza, Argentina nearly eight months later. He would be wearing a red net vest, jeans and a canvass hat, beneath which a black ponytail fell half way down his back. His smile beamed a welcome as the overnight bus from Buenos Aires drew to a stop. Bearded, not someone to wear high heels beside, a little chubby and a born joker, he proceeded to pull a face which would become all too familiar over the next seven weeks - head down, eyes lowered, lips pursed, his eyebrows seemed to do a little dance.

And so it was an Andean high priest and a middle-aged European woman set forth to activate the new feminine *ch'amas* for themselves and others.

Above: Burning my 'love' despacho at Puno ceremonial site

Ch'ama 1 - The Story
Aconcagua, Mendoza, Argentina

The first ch'ama corresponds with the root or base chakra, the adrenal glands which are responsible for fight or flight and issues concerning the lower limbs, as well as smell, hunger, security, belonging, identity and good judgement.

Apu had written to me about Aconcagua, the root *ch'ama* for the world, and the importance of our *Kundalini* activation ceremony to my health and well-being. I had visions of a huge energetic release - going up in smoke, frazzled and transformed beyond all recognition. In a way, that's what happened without my noticing, slowly and almost painlessly over the next six months. With Maria Moonstar's trip, my life had changed. My Peruvian experiences, including flying with the Condor and the ceremony of 'the here and now,' stayed with me and life became good.

Apu's warm, broad smile put me at ease. He sat, like a friendly beacon, looking out of the window towards my bus. He demanded my attention. After an international flight, a day touring Buenos Aires and an overnight bus ride I was exhausted. A violent thunder storm had lit up the vast unfamiliar landscape and sheet rain made for some anxious driving. I hadn't slept well. As I set foot on Mendoza, I was surprised to be back on this side of the world again so soon. We hugged and swapped accounts of our journeys. Apu had arrived before me and believed the wonderful and kind people he had met were a good omen for our trip. Picking up my rucksack with his own, he walked me to the next bus stop. After a short wait we set off for Uspallata, another two-hour drive where the wide open spaces and scrubland, the dusty streetscape, new-builds and outdoor café-eating reminded me of Queensland.

It was 10th December 2014, and the visit to our first *ch'ama* marking the beginning of our pilgrimage was two days off. Aconcagua is a mountain at the southern end of the Andes chain and is the seat of *Kundalini* energy. Its name is a Quechuan word meaning 'Stone Guardian.' At 6,962 metres it is the highest mountain outside of the Himalayas, and its southern wall one of the largest on Earth. While other connection points for the first *ch'ama* lie as far afield as Chile, Patagonia, Bolivia and Uruguay, Khon Kawan, the main doorway into the etheric city, is here. Our visit and offerings would serve to improve our sense of self and enable us to let go of the past.

Arriving at our wooden cabin earlier, we heard about a shaman and a spiritual community located thirty minutes away by car. We decided to visit the following day. Together we walked into town to get a flavour of rural Argentina. A delightful little restaurant sign offered free meals for any man accompanied by his wife and mistress. On the route back I gazed in my jetlagged way at the verdant green landscape with horses grazing. It seemed extraordinarily beautiful. Back at the pretty campsite, Apu sat calmly, his golden sun disc dangling round his neck, rucksacks and maps casually slung everywhere. He was preparing rice in huge quantities. The stray dogs would get most of it.

That night, sat in our wooden cabin, Apu suddenly said, 'When I look at you I see someone who fluctuates between a beautiful and powerful woman and a young child.' His brown eyes possessed an intense warmth and penetrating focus. "What do you feel? What do you want? What is your history?'

So I told him. As I spoke, sometimes I was sad, even in tears, and at other times I felt joyful or angry. First I explained my childhood on the farm, then my childhood illness, followed by blissful hours spent riding horses, my parents' divorce, relationships and exploring the world.

At eighteen months I was admitted to hospital, where I stayed for six months, one of the lucky ones sent home after ground-breaking steroid treatments for Stills disease. I experienced periods of fever, colourful hallucinations and paralysis. At times I couldn't see, found it hard to communicate or floated painlessly above my body. For most of my early childhood I was immobile, carried around or sat bouncing in the kitchen doorway. When I was finally released from hospital, my mum let me walk too soon and my condition flared up again. Petrified, she kept me off my feet for nearly two years, until I went to school. Subconsciously, I kept my legs heavy so I wouldn't get sick again.

I told Apu how a journey woman in Pizac had taken the whole illness episode away, as if it never happened. Poetically, she saw a small group of ancient Quechuan people walking in the snow-capped mountains, with a happy baby wrapped in a blanket, to a ceremony. The group entered a 'light' cave made of crystal with sacred symbols on the floor to anoint the baby as a high priest. This baby, a hermaphrodite, was in perfect health, balanced and content. It was very special, conscious of its body, the mountains, sentient beings, the Earth and cosmos – connected with everything. It was as if I, as the baby, could return to the idyllic pre-verbal days before the illness.

As babies, all five of us spent long hours in the garden, our prams strategically placed under an apple tree for diversion and shelter. Years later we climbed that tree, built tree houses and zip wires down to the paddling pool, and kept tabs on the men's urinal in the pub next door. My childhood was idyllic in many ways: fun, easy and extremely communal. There were always cousins and friends at the dinner table and sometimes farmers negotiating a business deal over copious tumblers of whiskey. We built tunnels out of straw bales, played cat and mouse or roamed the countryside on horseback.

In other ways there was an absence, mostly on my dad's side. He didn't get involved in our upbringing, never attending sports days or attending school concerts. I have a vivid memory of holding his large hand in the bottom field below Etsome Terrace when I was four or five. Dad was a man of his times, hardwired to keep his emotions under lock and key – no doubt a by-product of being a much-loved youngest son, his public school upbringing and his part in a fatal bike accident as a teenager. Dad, to my eyes, seemed big, generous and wonderful company. I adored him, emulated him and consistently chose men like him for my partner.

Mum opened a playgroup to provide me with a little stimulation, but being older than the other kids and essentially immobile I tended towards passive observation. Descriptions of me as a young child lean towards words like 'moody' and 'solitary.' I often disappeared to my favourite spot at the top of the orchard where the farmyard wall was just low enough to peer over to the animals and see Doug, the farmhand, going about his work. I found it hard to join in with my siblings or school friends. Jack, my pony, was my saving grace, bringing me back into the world. Not the same world as most young girls inhabited, but a world I loved and which seemed familiar.

Even as a baby, my mum said I was special. I thought that meant something really special but actually she meant 'different.' Now, after years working in the disability field, I would pinpoint that difference to dyslexia or being on the autistic spectrum; or maybe heightened sensitivity or post traumatic shock disorder due to my months in hospital. Whatever the cause, eccentricity runs in the family. I recognise our ability to focus on a passion, our relative disinterest in money and possessions, a determination to stick up for the underdog, and a certain fearlessness.

I was special in other ways. In early grammar school I spent hours in my bedroom along with Marianne, talking to the spirits on our Ouija board. We had a complex arrangement with a glass, bits of paper with letters of the alphabet, numbers and words like 'yes' and 'no' written on them, as well as personal spirit guides whom we could ask questions and obtain answers from. These would come via messages spelt out on the board and 'knocking'. I can't remember now if the knocks were the glass on the table or the table on the floor but recall my parents shouting up the narrow stairwell to shut us up. The sound had to be pretty loud to get through those old farmhouse walls.

I was perhaps thirteen when I crept out of the farmhouse late one night and cycled up Etsome Terrace to the top field. It was a twenty-minute journey, undertaken with a saddle balanced on the handlebars and reins flapping in the wind. I was alone, and hadn't told a soul. I had set myself this challenge, and was determined to follow it through. I lay my bike on its side and Jack came trotting towards me, his brown and white body and thick white tail emerging from the murky darkness. I tacked him up and we set off down the steep hill.

To get to the moors I needed to pass the Adams farm, after which there was no habitation for miles. I felt fine until we veered left onto a different stretch of road, leaving the farm buildings behind. Then the terror set in. There was at least another fifteen minutes to go, deeper into the darkness, with only withy trees and ditch water for company. All the way I thought aloud, pushing Jack onwards until the moment he first set his hoof on the moor. I wanted to discover if witches were out there casting spells at midnight. We blinked into the darkness together, and the only sounds that reached us came from ourselves. Then we turned and galloped back as if possessed. Down the eerie track, over Etsome Bridge, flying up the hill with hoofs sharp against the tarmac and devils at our back.

And then there was that dream. A week before my university finals, a fortnight at the outside. I woke one night with the sure feeling that my boyfriend was seeing a red-headed older woman. I asked him directly. He said yes. As if that wasn't distressing enough, I was woken two or three times a night experiencing strange bone-rattling sensations. I would sit bolt upright in bed vibrating all over. 'Are you having sex into the small hours?' I asked him.

Apu listened intently, nodded and returned to uploading photos on his Facebook page. He read my energy but my words were more or less irrelevant to his task. He had no intention of getting bogged down in the emotionally-laden description of my issues. From the beginning of our relationship I noticed he was usually polite. Then, if you had not understood him, he ignored you and finally said it how it was. The subject was closed. His concern was to change my energy matrix and transform my sense of identity beyond the current 'me' – and he intended to do it his way.[8]

Aware that Andean philosophy maintains that we need a strong sense of self to survive and feel secure and at home, I pondered what actions Apu would take. When parts of us are split off, usually due to trauma, we are left weakened and dispirited. It is the job of the shaman to restore us and this is achieved by venturing into the spirit world. This is a complex, multidimensional land needing careful navigation. Maybe Apu was proposing to venture there on my behalf, and bring back any soul parts that were still missing after my illness, an ancient shamanic tradition.

The next morning was warm as we travelled by taxi out of the built-up area, arriving unannounced at the spiritual community, where we were received very generously and invited to tea. A grey haired, bearded, trim, casually-dressed man approached us and invited us to sit. This was a master called Emilio, guide and teacher of a group of young people. Emilio and Apu talked, exchanging stories and checking shamanic

This page: Apu meditating, looking out over Uspallata

credentials whilst his students came and went to a background of chicken, bee, pig, goat and horse sounds. After a while, a man in the community spoke about a sacred place with special energies fifteen minutes away. Emilio invited us to a guided meditation.

Emilio called in the four directions then sang a beautiful melody with three women from the community. We were invited to stand and connect with our inner light then drop back into the arms of a singer, having shed an 'issue' and reconnected with *Pachamama*. Apu suddenly felt the need to move while Emilio continued talking. 'His voice frequency varies a lot, and in my head the word *Merk, Merk, MERK* started to resonate. I cannot understand what is happening. I feel bad.' After the meditation, and many hours of hospitality, we took our leave. By this point, Apu seemed a little restored.

On day two, climbing the rugged terrain of the local sacred mountain where Christians walk the fourteen Stations of the Cross during holy week, Apu was still trying to understand why he had not been able to finish the meditation. The word *Merk* echoed in his head. The sacred mountain was steep, the day hot and the view over Uspallata superb. As we rested from climbing, I reflected on the meaning of the first *ch'ama* and Apu's words. 'The lesson of the first *ch'ama* is to find your path in life, to become surer of who you are and become anchored in this world – in this life and on your path.' No mean feat! I needed to take responsibility for my own healing and self-development, find out why I had come into this world the way I had, unravel the issues I had invited along my path and understand my gifts, passions and shortcomings – in other words, my vocation or *raison d'etre*.

Tomorrow would be a big day, our visit to Apu Aconcagua, the highest mountain of the female part of the Earth, *Pachamama*. I hoped to find some answers.

In the foothills, our bus negotiated each bend whilst we sat back and enjoyed the view. Apu suggested I relax and feel the energy of the mountain. 'Let it come slowly.' Arriving at Inca Bridge with its spa waters and mineral salts, Apu told me the little town's story. The child of a great king had once fallen gravely ill. Informed that healing waters lay close to the mountains of Aconcagua, the king searched until he spied medicinal hot springs the other side of the river. However, after heavy rainfall the water was extremely treacherous. The king despaired. Then his soldiers divined a solution, positioning themselves on top of each other to form a bridge enabling him to cross and heal his child. Because of the soldiers' love for their king, their bodies were petrified to remind humanity that when a leader is good to his people, they will sacrifice their lives for him. Thus, the first *ch'ama* also represents sacrifice for a good cause.

Arriving at the park entrance we bought tickets and set about getting permission to bring in our offerings – flowers, peaches, avocados, red wine and Bacardi.

Disappointingly, the park ranger would not allow us, even though Apu was an Andean priest coming to make an offering to *Pachamama*. The ranger continued to formally resist but eventually relented, 'Don't leave anything behind. Have a nice day.' We took it as tacit approval to continue with the offerings we had. With a quick nod of his head Apu said goodbye and we started our pilgrimage to the sacred lands.

We passed lagoons where Apu pointed out an Andean duck without a partner. Unusual, since they normally mate for life. At the second lagoon, Horcones, we stood to admire Aconcagua. 'Look closely at Apu Aconcagua's face.' Starting with the pyramid at his throat, I looked up and saw his chin, nose and forehead and an indent for an eye. A man's face was visible in the mountain side. To our side were huge stones, 'Wandering Blocks', an example of the strength of the water, wind and glaciers working together.

On the banks of the river descending directly from Aconcagua, Apu decided on a place in the dry river bed to make our offering. The setting was beautiful and a flock of tiny birds surrounded us, coming almost close enough to touch. I was horrified to discover that the battery in my camera was flat, but Apu calmed me. 'Feel with your heart, do not think in the rational Western way you have been taught. Live in the moment and focus intently on what is happening around you during our first *ch'ama* ceremony — not on taking photographs.'

Then something strange happened. I became aware of the sparse vegetation. *Yellow firewood, yareta* and *goat horn* pervaded my senses. On the wind were memories of spotted sandpipers, mountain rats, European hares and Torrente duck. As Apu focused on our *despacho* ceremony I gazed at his hands whilst they worked. Within minutes I had entered into another world.

Above: Inca Bridge

This page: The face of Aconcagua

I was conscious of a dark coloured band of thick metal around my hips along with a plug of Hoocha[9] or heavy energy at the base of my spine which kept me rooted to the spot. The mmm... sound resonated deeply in my body. The metal band loosened and fell to the ground. Again and again I forced the energy up and down my spinal channel, sticky and slow. The thick plug loosened, dispersed and transformed into a host of small dots located in my flesh and in all of my vital organs. Eventually it reshaped in the form of a light blue, wafer thin wisp of material lodged in my left hip, like a healing blanket.

Birds and animals seemed extremely close to me. I saw the eyes of a falcon, and a condor was with me indicating something important was going to happen. Owls flew by in unusual patterns, multitudes of salmon leapt up a waterfall and a grey wolf with yellow eyes was my protector.

As the energy shifted I became a giant[10] striding across the mountain landscape. I journeyed up and down the height of Aconcagua and ate up vast tracts of land in the valley. My lithe, slender legs took enormous steps, travelling its ridge to neighbouring mountains along the Southern Andes with ease. Animal-like and instinctual, I felt the giant brought much needed chaos and destruction in its wake, as it confidently navigated this new and unfamiliar environment.

Before I returned to normal reality there was a glimpse of joyfulness and I felt the power of a snake in the moments of shedding its skin. The mountain landscape appeared to be shrouded in a web of thin, blue light. Afterwards, my legs needed to run forever, on and on. Apu seemed to be somehow untouchable so I sat on the rocky riverbed, silently shaking, and as my legs ran and shook, pleasant but unfamiliar sensations returned to my body. A potent shift had occurred.

Apu had entered a trance and later described seven small birds or angelic beings approaching him. They seemed tame and unafraid to be near us. One assumed human form without changing its height and said,

> *Welcome to Khon Kawan, Apu.*

Immediately, the others assumed human form and spoke in turn,

> *I am the guardian of Uritorco hill in Cordoba, one of the entrances to the city Etherica, the city of Erks. We met during your last visit to that land.*

> *I come from Patagonia. I am the guardian of the gate to the city of the Caesars, as named by the temple monks, one of the entrances to Khon Kawan.*

> *I am from Aurora, in Uruguay, another doorway to Khon Kawan.*

> *I am the guardian of Horcones in the Valley of Elqui in Chile. Welcome.*
>
> *I am from the Tunupa volcano in the saltpan of Uyuni. Bolivia extends its greetings to you.*
>
> *From the mines of Wanda I have come on many missions, summoned to welcome you.*

The first was most notable. It grew in size and in a powerful voice said,

> *My name is Merk, priest and guardian of Khon Kawan, also known in Argentina as the city of Isidris. My divine and* Pachamama*-energised compliments to you. I bid you welcome.*

At this moment, Apu was in touch with his feminine side.

> *You have reached the time to prove you are entitled to your name and have embodied the feminine. It is the beginning of a new era. Jenny will enable you to cross through the* ch'amas *of Pachamama and you must guide her towards the new age. Along your way the* Q'eros, Asachos, Willoq, Ayarachis, Italaques *and other Andean peoples will dispense knowledge, embody the spiritual example and help bring about change. Welcome. More information will be given at the other* ch'amas.

Then Apu was invited to cross the bridge. He followed obediently, though he wondered if it was a good idea. Giving a backward glance, he saw his body on its knees before me and realized it was his etheric body crossing the bridge. More confident now, soon he was approaching a welcoming city of gleaming temples.

Master Merk nodded,

> *This is Khon Kawan, the great etheric temple where ancestral knowledge is stored; some visitors call the city Isidris, the first energy centre of the feminine part of mother Earth, the continent that before the arrival of the Spanish the natives called Abya Yala which we now know as America.*
>
> *Jenny and yourself have been welcomed and initiated on the journey of the seven* ch'amas *of Pachamama. Remember your training as a* Paqo *(Andean priest). Everything must be carried out simply and easily. Theory is not in our path, we progress through action and example. We are not guided by the mind or emotion, rather the intelligence of the heart. This must be the principle that you, your travelling companion, and all those you take on your path must honour. This is only the beginning of a process that will culminate in June 2060. You will gain more information at the different* ch'amas *of Pachamama. Now go back to Jenny and continue your journey.*

Returning to his physical body, Apu continued with the ceremony, filled with new energy. We buried the offerings and built an *Apacheta*, a small tower of stones used by Andean priests as a sign of an important event or to mark that a change of consciousness has occurred. It was then we noticed that the weather had changed, with the wind blowing in the opposite direction. Retracing the mountain path, a number of omens and signs presented themselves. First, Apu spotted a hummingbird unusually high up. Then he saw a horse-head image in a small piece of stone at the track edge and rabbit-like creatures high up the mountainside.

We continued the one kilometre walk over the Park headland to Inca Bridge. The energy here was different, somehow heavier, in comparison to the rarefied, pure air at Aconcagua. So instead of staying the night as planned we caught the bus to Uspallata. 'You were radiant,' Apu told me, 'your inner self underwent a major change.' I felt a wonderful lightness, joy and a seam of heat run up my right-hand side. The *Kundalini* energy wasn't just for me, however. Apu said he was leaving the past behind and only taking forward good experiences.

The next day we took the bus to Valpariso, Chile, then north towards La Serena in the valley of Elqui and on to the Peruvian border. It was the start of a forty-hour road journey to the second *ch'ama* in Lake Titicaca. Mostly, we slept and looked out of the window; occasionally we talked and every so often stopped and visited somewhere.

We might have had a lucky escape at Santiago. Arriving late at night, we were in search of a hotel bed when an apparently harmless Italian-speaker offered us

Above: Market flowers

Above: Market groceries

accommodation. His energy didn't seem right from the start. After twenty minutes of waiting for transport to his hotel, we began to feel anxious. Apu called me aside, we picked up our luggage and left the man standing alone on the sidewalk.

He was right, the atmosphere was heavy and it didn't feel safe. The next day, a huge market lifted our spirits and we fingered through the various wares for hours, vendors delightedly telling me I could ship goods home or that I looked resplendent in one of their straw hats. Later we ate traditional food, dishes loaded with chips and meat in a restaurant lined with photos and knick-knacks. An old man in a jaunty black cap played guitar. The day was fabulous.

Ch'ama 2 - Breakthrough
Amantani, Lake Titicaca, Peru

The second ch'ama corresponds with the sacral chakra, the matrix responsible for reproduction and the lymphatic system which disposes the body's rubbish, as well as issues of taste, creativity, balance of the masculine and feminine, sexual intimacy, desire and tenderness.

From Santiago we headed to Le Serena where we stopped opposite the boat-shaped lighthouse facing the beach, now a restaurant with pirate waiters in the ramparts. We visited the craft markets and viewed an ornate church bell tower and then walked and kept walking – perhaps for ten hours in total. In those hot backstreets we made a huge, perambulatory square around the vast town. All the while Apu was telling me, 'Feel your feet on the pavement. Connect.' When I was disconnected and struggled to cope, he pulled a face or shocked me suddenly from behind to bring me back to the present. He said ominously that he was working on my behalf and would do 'whatever is necessary.'

As we wandered, we talked. I asked Apu about healing and he told me he used energetic healing techniques from the Andean tradition. For Indians, everything in life is energy. 'Sickness' itself is only lazy energy. When I move this lazy energy it's a healing process.' In the Andean way of looking at the world, everything is simple and easy. For example, Apu's master explained gas colic as 'energy in the stomach or intestines which brings increasing pain until it is moved.' The solution? 'Take a pill, or some herbs (tea), or move the gas through your mouth or bottom.'

Apu encourages people to be happy. 'This is part of my work. Sick people are not so happy, so part of my job is to give them happiness.[11] If I give them the good energies I have, maybe in receiving them they will notice the good energies they have in themselves.' As a healer, he doesn't overly dwell on the results of his healings. 'Energies are the best cure for sick people. When you live in the here and now, you open the channel to the great masters and goddesses to give to the sick people who need your help. Why think about what's good or bad? *Pachamama* lives life in the moment, in the here and now.'

My mind wandered. His words reminded me how traumatic events can become lodged in our cells and unless reprogrammed are relived with a different cast on another stage — or manifest themselves as disease. The energies become stuck. As we walked, I revisited old dramas stored at apparently random sites in my body — the top of my right palm contained painful memories of receiving gifts from people who pitied me; my throat held a memory of laughter at my youthful efforts in love; my head and ears retained a fear that my lover might not return from the Troubles; my buttocks held feelings of anger, bitterness and betrayal by myself and others. Most of all, the memory of my mother's anxiety about letting me walk too early was stored in my legs.

After a few hours we arrived at a small cafe just off the beach. The interior was air-conditioned. In my mind, as I ordered drinks, Gaea a course facilitator in London said, 'Stand up! Don't let yourself be distracted, don't pay any attention to the others, they aren't worried about you. They're happily doing their own thing. You don't like the attention, do you?' Gaea rubbed my chest roughly. 'Ah, you gorgeous woman, you might not like the attention but you still have to breathe.' I felt a growing awareness of a pain down the side of my left leg, nothing unbearable but a consciousness whenever I was seated or lying on the floor. Suddenly there was a flash on the right side of my head and some minutes afterwards a sensation, something falling out of the corner of my eye like a heavy teardrop of mercury. The pain moved. Time passed. I had no idea how long for, as I sucked the air in and sighed it back out again. At first it felt like pins and needles in one of my hands and then a creeping Michelin man sensation, the edges of my body disappearing into a wider space, full of bubbles or energy. All but my right leg and head entered this weird and wonderful void, where the edges of reality blurred.

Carrying our order into the heat outside, we drank with a dry thirst and started walking again. Apu continued, 'In a person with cancer, the energies have taken many years to accumulate. *What about a sick baby who hasn't had time to accumulate bad energies?* you might ask. Such a spirit has lived other lives and created karma and agreed to come to this life with this cancer.' Had I agreed to come back and contract Stills Disease as a small child?

During hypnosis in England, the complexity of our minds' workings was first revealed to me. Emma took me back to when I was a child of two. Asked which part of my body benefited from eating stodgy food, I named my legs. 'Heavy legs mean I can't move, and if I don't move I won't get sick again.' I had an inkling that my weight was connected to my childhood illness, but I hadn't realised the practical nature of this programming I had carried with me ever since.

Apu tapped me on the shoulder. I had gone off into my own world again. We walked on and I asked about his tools. 'They are similar to Reiki, but in the Andean tradition we move the energies from the energetic mouth (the navel — our mouth

This page: Travelling across the Peruvian Altiplano

while *in utero*) by putting our hands on different parts of the body.' He explained that to complete a healing he uses other energies – those of plants, animals and powerful tools. 'My master told me that a healer's energy accounts for 70% of a healing, and pills, plants and minerals make up the remaining 30%.' Other priests and shamans use tobacco smoke to suck out negative energy. Singing and whistling, they call the plant spirits to their aid and use the fourteen energetic points of the body (as recognised in acupuncture) as a diagnostic and healing tool. Plant medicines like *Ayahuasca* and San Pedro are commonly used to help. 'I am a San Pedro master', Apu said. 'Maybe you would like a San Pedro healing one day?'

'For happiness it is important to make sure your energy is clean and grounded by releasing negative energy into the earth.' As Apu talked, Minty came into my mind.[12] He was a broad-set piebald cob back in England. Suddenly he went soft all over, dropped his head, closed his eyes and let his back leg relax. 'Is Minty going to fall over?' I asked. 'No he's fine, he's just resting, he's relaxed,' Shelley replied. Like my mount I turned off, accepting of my lot. It felt like work to me, letting the energy flow through me, doing nothing, observing micro-second changes. The combination of concentration on the one hand and a sense of nothingness on the other was familiar from my rehabilitation work.

One horse and rider could not bear to be near other people. The two kept their distance. Suddenly, a ball of energy fired out from them as they walked towards us. It was palpable, a dense, swirling light rapidly travelling down the centre of the arena. A boundary had been crossed. As quickly as the energy was shot out it was absorbed and transmuted. Not a noticeable flicker from either Minty or I – but if I felt it, I'm sure he did. Beneath me, Minty was quietly licking and chewing in agreement and recognition of the change in their energy signature. The true extent of the magic revealed itself from then on in. The rider on her Andalusian horse tolerated increasing physical closeness from Minty and I, and by the end of the horse whispering workshop they were trotting side by side with anyone who cared to join them.

Apu noticed I was not connected with him. We reached a suburban shopping centre and sat in a cafe balcony overlooking a car park. Finally, he imitated my disassociation and childhood tantrums and I felt his absence, his disquiet. My body reacted violently and I rushed off to the toilet. After this much-needed break, we walked on and Apu described his wonderful approach to life. 'Be happy. Life is simple.' The outside mirrors the inside and energy reflects energy. 'If we give out sadness, we receive it in return. The same holds for happiness.' Focus on the outward manifestation of your internal energy, operate in the moment and trust your instincts. The 'new feminine path' of harmony and equilibrium requires a break with our old ways of thinking and being to be fully understood.' Logic and structured thinking need to make way for feeling and living in the here and now. As we travelled to the second *ch'ama*, this was Apu's message.

After Le Serena we crossed the Peruvian border and the sandy heights and seemingly barren tracks of land of the Peruvian Altiplano in a series of minicabs. As we climbed, my head began to ache and I felt nauseous. I fell asleep struggling to cope in the small space at such a high altitude but woke to find us close to Puno. Much to my delight we were passing colourfully-dressed women with long black plaits down their backs and men in *chullos*, multicoloured knitted hats. The cheapest transport was little three-wheeler bikes with tarpaulin roofs and backseats big enough for two. Our first port of call was the market, walking through narrow crowded alleys to buy *despacho* offerings, llama foetuses, *K'intus* (coca leaves) and red and white flower offerings for our second *ch'ama* trip.

A *despacho* consists of a large piece of white paper, otherwise known as an envelope of dreams, folded into nine squares. Inside are packages containing small sachets of sugar (love), rice (abundance), llama fat (energy in its purest form), little figurines (male and female, balance), gold and silver paper (wisdom), red beans (night and day) and stars (brothers and sisters). Red wine representing the blood of *Pachamama* and white wine, *pisco* or vodka is poured on the earth as an offering to the mountain spirits. During a *despacho* ceremony Apu wished his prayer into the *K'intus*, telling them what we wanted.

The second *chakra* connects with our emotions, our ability to be flexible and flow, to give and to receive. It is linked to the throat and our ability to communicate, relating to balance and enjoyment in all relationships – particularly creative and sexual ones. The second *ch'ama*, and the sexual centre of *Pachamama* is 'the Monastery of the Seven Rays.' It is the name of the etheric city related to this *ch'ama*, but is also a physical place, Kuichi Marka in Peru, located below Lake Titicaca. We planned to hold our ceremony on the Island of Amantani on the Peruvian side of the Lake. Other connection points include the Island of the Sun on the Bolivian side and Aramu Muru, among others.

Apu tells a story of how his master came to enter the etheric city through the Aramu Muru inter-dimensional doorway and returned with a golden sun disc. Along with *Paq'os, Pampa Misayocs, Alto Misayocs, Kolla Yatiris, Kallahuayas* and other Andean priests and healers, he was summoned to Puno to celebrate the arrival of *Pachacuti*, a solar day for the Andeans that lasts approximately 1,000 years. After seven days of meetings and conferences, he felt the need to visit Don Salustiano Mamani, a respected *Kolla Yatiri*, to say goodbye. Together they entered the spirit valley and headed towards a mountain in which an enormous door (seven by seven metres) had been carved. There, his master said, 'It seemed as if the rock was getting softer and softer, until suddenly it opened up and there was a tunnel that allowed my body to go through. I wanted to cry with emotion because what was in front of my eyes was so beautiful.'

We set off to the second *ch'ama* with arms full of flowers, *pisco*, wine and gifts of cooking oil for our island hosts. Amantani is the second biggest of the islands on

Lake Titicaca. Our boat chugged along slowly. It was warm and pleasant motoring through the reed beds with the clouds mirrored in the water, and left to my own devices I reminisced. The morning disappeared, the only interruptions coming from the Uros ferrymen attending their work. Apu was preparing our *despacho* ceremony and had located a possible site for his healing centre on the wild headland of the Capachica peninsula. I was thinking of an ex-boyfriend someone had mentioned out of the blue. I hadn't heard from him for four years, yet here he was popping into my mind on the very day of our sexual healing ceremony. Images flitted through my mind – my pony Jack hot and sweaty beneath me as we hunted witches on the moor; my mother reading me *Swallows and Amazons* on the twilit banks of the Parret. Messages related to this *ch'ama*, perhaps.

The boat having docked, my senses were assaulted with terraces, houses and gardens vital with fruit, crops and animals. We climbed the steep path to our lodgings to be warmly greeted by our host Nicasio, dressed in his traditional black hat and jacket. His wife Inés, was in her *pollera*, a white shirt and embroidered jacket, and she had prepared a special lunch of roasted guinea pig and quinoa on the open hearth in Apu's honour. I found a wonderful purity and freshness in the behaviour of the Island people. It is a rare privilege to be in such company. They have a willingness to share, time to tell stories in the evenings, a sense that nothing is too much trouble. Coupled with this is a great feeling of support and community – people helping each other, parents in love with their children, children in love with their parents and husbands and wives overtly in love with each other.

Later that afternoon, our sacral ceremony at the shaman's site below the temples of *Pachamama* and *Pachatata* was quite extraordinary. Under my breath I intoned the Rune sounds and meanings for my name and chanted the individual sounds, JENN..I..FER, JENN..I..FER, JENN..I..FER, over and over again. J for Jera and cycles of natural growth and change, E for Ehwaz representing horse energy and shamanic journeying and double N for Nadiz and having my basic needs met (shelter, food and love). Next, I or Isa concerns being in the moment, followed by F for Fehu representing fulfilment, wealth and personal power, another E which doubles the power of horse energy and shamanic journeying and lastly R for Raido which again has a horse association and means shamanic journeying but also represents rhythm and vibration, movement and travel.

As birds flew overhead in a circle crowning our ceremony and we were accompanied by a band of angels (musicians playing far-off in the hills) I lost myself in the moment. Beginning to trust,

Above: Taking the sheep up to the high pastures

Above: Apachetas at the shaman ceremonial site

I looked and listened for the signs. A friend appeared to arrive and rise to the skies on a witch's broomstick carrying a small medicine bottle and a piece of boulder opal. He was dressed in a red and yellow superman outfit. I drank the medicine and visions came. First a colourful parrot close to my face, a group of black and white penguins in the distance, the eyes and nose of a mouse and the fuzzy, soft feathers of a bird being fed by its mother. I remembered the orphaned lambs we kept in our airing cupboard at the farmhouse and the old reaping machine and workmen in their long, dirty beige coats tied around the waist with binder twine.

There were many steps leading down into a deep cellar in the bowels of a Scottish castle, where a plug needed to be dislodged to let water flow in. I walked in the terraces and high mountains of Peru, became the bark of a tree and then a cloudy cell moving through my body and a bird soaring high in the skies. There was a glimpse of a green dragon. It was hiding and only came out on special occasions. Three parallel lines, like telephone wires, led into the future.

When I looked around me the landscape had changed to Silbury Hill, near Avebury. My friend landed and talked to the goddess who lives there. She was crouching like

This page: Our sacral ch'ama ceremony

a woman in labour, her huge belly nudging the sky. 'Where is your life force, where have you been all these years?' he asked her. 'Please focus and pay attention. You need to gain new knowledge and let your innate creativity shine.'

On the walk back Apu rewarded me. He placed two small black gnarled rocks in my hand - one for the feminine and one for the masculine. He told me to hold them and keep them warm as they were important symbols for my coming journey. This ceremony was dedicated to my mother in particular, and to mothers in general, their ultimate creativity in giving birth to new life. It was as if our *despacho* created a microcosm of the three Andean worlds and all the sweetness and light contained within them. In so doing, our ceremony represented and re-balanced my mother's world. Recently she had struggled with the deaths of three close friends in quick succession. It had left a gap in her life. Apu went into a deep trance and connected with her energy, shifting what needed to be shifted, recreating her future.

I have been aware of my mother's healing powers since I was a girl. She would sit with her hands cupped around whichever part of our body was scratched or bruised. Indeed, she sometimes went as far as to take out her sewing kit to mend broken skin, carefully knotting the cotton thread at the conclusion of her work. Once, she even sewed up the gaping bloody hole between two toes on my right foot after I had inadvertently stood on a stray pitchfork. I limped across the garden, the pitchfork held gingerly in one hand, the prong still embedded. Dad sat me down and pulled it out and then mum went to fetch her sewing kit. There were few tears on my part, and little or no condolences, just a perfunctory operation before I was back on my feet. Years later, I learnt that my throat *chakra* meridian,[13] which begins between the toes, had been stabbed and scarred that day.

One summer holiday, when my mum was bored with the farm routine and needed to escape, she took my younger brother Tim and I camping on the River Parret. We set up house down by the water and within a stone's throw of a farm in order to procure our daily milk, fresh and creamy straight from a cow. By day we played with the clay from John Leech's pottery or walked for miles to Muchelney Abbey to see beautiful angels on the powder blue church roof. Mum paddled us up river in the canoe left for us by Reg Potts, the 'aunty' who happily carried me around Somerton in the days of my childhood illness. At twilight, in a theatrical voice, she read us the next chapter from *Swallows and Amazons*. We woke to swans gliding past silently on the misty waters and the deep mysteriousness of the Somerset moorlands.

Mum was unorthodox in her youth. She set up a playgroup to keep me off my feet and entertained as a pre-school child, then a youth club for bored local teenagers in a small country town. She later sat on the Parish Council. She had always wanted children and filled the farm house not only with the five of us but also hoards of cousins, friends and foster children. On top of this, she cared for her husband's aged grandparents until they passed away. I vividly remember her setting me tasks as a child

— make a phone call home from the red telephone box, find this address, buy a loaf of bread from the baker's, wash the car for twenty pence.

Born an identical twin, my mother has a capacity for telepathy and compassion which engenders a special closeness with all those around her, myself included. She visited me in hospital as a toddler, a daily trip of forty miles whilst pregnant and with three young children at home. A deep connection was formed between us in those early days. We still spend hours together on creative projects - *trompe l'oeils* on my house walls and quirky gifts for family and friends.

Apu and I were not alone in our lodgings. Another visitor from the mainland, transporting books as part of an educational program for the children of the island, proved a lively dinner guest. He talked in Spanish and English, interpreting back and forth for the group. He was determined in his cause, the need to educate children.

That evening, Apu came to my simple room and performed a flower cleansing ceremony. This forms part of a priest's armoury. Before a cleansing, he explained, if someone has a piercing or is even wearing a hair-band, the water or vapour of the herbs used in a *temascal* (a type of sweat lodge) will also penetrate these items, and thus when removed, part of the cleansing will be lost. To receive all of the ceremony's benefits one is advised to do it unclothed. Everyone must do what they feel is right, as I did.

Morning broke to find me humming an old Somerset tune.

> *Where be that blackbird to?*
> *I know where he be*
> *He be in that wurzel tree and I be after he*
> *Blackbird I'll have 'ee.*[14]

It was sad to leave the wonderful energies of Amantani. Whilst stepping onto our boat, Apu greeted another powerful shaman who was leading a group of spiritual tourists. As we untied the ropes, this man came to the edge of the wharf and said, 'Goodbye, Jenny.' His presence was extraordinary — he had an all-seeing look in his eye. Back on the lake once more, we stopped at a sacred outcrop and disembarked to perform another sacral *ch'ama* ceremony amidst the winds and breaking waves. It was surreal, out there in the middle of the lake, balanced on a handful of big rocks giving our ceremonial offering to a blow-hole. It was a powerful place. The energy penetrated my body and united me with the sky, the lake and its depths, allowing me to find a deep peace.

On the boat ride back to Puno, Apu spoke about the sacred lake's place in history as the cradle of no less than three Andean civilizations — the Pucara, Tihuanaco and then the Incas. The Lake is an enormous body of water, 103 miles long containing

Above: The Sacred Rock

more than thirty islands. It is home to not just a medley of birds and fish – Carachi, Mauri, Ispi, Suche or Catfish – but also the descendants of Peru's oldest ethnic group, the Uros, and Sun Island the birthplace of the Inca civilization.

Apu also told me the delightful story of Quesintu and Umantu, two young girls who lived on Lake Titicaca. One day the fish started to disappear and hunger came to the inhabitants of the lake. Their prayers went unanswered, and Quesintu and Umantu saw the sad faces of the fishermen. One morning when swimming the girls were taken by Chuquilla[15] and presumed dead, but that very night Chuquilla re-emerged and left them on the shore, alive. Slowly, the girls' bellies started to swell and eventually they gave birth in the sacred waters. Quesinto gave birth to fish with scales and Umanto to fish without scales and soon the fishermen started to fill their nets. When the girls passed away, an enormous monolith (later destroyed by the fanatical priests of the Inquisition) was carved in their honour. Stone carvers from the region made sure the girls were remembered by carving their images into the pillars of Qosqo cathedral.

Back in Puno, whilst eating a Chinese meal we met Don José, a specialist in medicinal plants, rituals and aura-reading – as well as a shaman friend of Apu. Having shared our meal, he agreed to make me a power tool. A supremely quiet, calm man, the energy coming from him was almost electric. In Apu's altar room, surrounded by thousands of sacred artefacts and shrunken skulls with a lone mattress in the centre, I was mesmerised. Don José prayed over the coca leaves, the fur of a Puma, a condor feather and 'lucky' beans – which he then held to my third eye to grant me a wish. Don José told me to keep the little marmalade-sized jar with its blue chequered top close to me and to hold it to my forehead whenever seeking guidance and insight. He made another to keep my mum safe, as well.

At Puno, the spirit valley beckoned once more and we revisited the Aramu Muru doorway with Apu's singing bowls. I bought some artwork from Mosho, Puno's most famous artist, and children joined us for our ceremony on the sacred 'back' of Puno, called Cerrito Huajsapata. Remembering my coca leaf reading, I wondered if I was any closer to opening myself up to love. Should I write, make inroads towards healthier living, perhaps move to Peru or Central America and fly in my heart and mind? One thing was certain, I had revisited the power of energies — both my own and that of the pure Island people on Amantani, the 'electric' shaman, the artist and the children.

I left Lake Titicaca and Puno on the bus to Qosqo and the third *ch'ama*. We drove via Pukara, an ancient civilisation from 1600 BC, La Raya, whose highest point reaches 4,335 metres above sea level, Raqchi, the temples of Wiracocha and Andahuaylillas and the church of San Pedro, Llamada la Sixtina de América. Apu would not return to Puno, his home-town, until the Virgin of the Candelaria Festival in the Altiplano in early February. I wasn't sure when and if I would ever return. On the way I received a message from my late father which I was keen to share with him. It had come to me *en route* to Qosqo. In the church of San Pedro — his namesake — he whispered that he wanted me to donate money on his behalf to help establish a healing centre to provide warmth, shelter and renewed health for anyone in need.

Ch'ama 3 - Embodiment
Killarumiyoq, Qosqo, Peru

The third ch'ama corresponds with the solar plexus chakra, the pancreas which is responsible for metabolism, sight, prosperity, motivation, will and power, self-assertion, taking responsibility for our own lives and accommodating differences.

When my tourist bus drew up in Qosqo it was a little disconcerting to see Apu at the bus stop accompanied by a woman. She seemed glued to his side as if they had known each other a long time. Vera, I learned later, was able to channel what she called 'dolphin energy' and was a beautiful singer, travelling on what she termed a 'spirit-led' tour with limited funds. A mutual friend in Chile had put her in touch with Apu and she had turned up at his family shop just half an hour before my bus was due. From the beginning there was financial high drama with Vera – lost or stolen money, missing purses, lost bank cards. She never seemed to have enough.

Qosqo sits at the head of the Sacred Valley, the 'Empire of the Four Directions of the World' or Tawantinsuyo, and the city of Qosqo (Cusco) is built in the shape of its totem animal – the Puma. Legend has it that the city was established at the place a golden staff sank into the ground when the Incas left Lake Titicaca. The surrounding land and cityscapes contain fabulous astronomical observatories and experimental crop centres. A myth recalls how of four brothers sent by their god, the Sun, to found Qosqo, only one survived. This man murdered the others and their wives. By the time he arrived at the city, he found it already populated and taught the people how to farm and undertake domestic activities. He became the first Inca king, Ayar Manko or Manco Capac.

The day after I arrived in Qosqo we wandered the city under the guidance of Apu. In the streets we met *el puma* and *la serpiente*. The Incas built secret, helpful messages into both the natural surroundings and the huge building blocks of their sacred buildings. We shopped for handmade boots and had our photo taken beside a covert Indian representation of their God, Ekeko, who represents good luck, prosperity and *Avundancia* (abundance).

If I was surprised to have Vera alongside us, I said nothing. Apu continued in his affable manner. Sitting on a café balcony overlooking Qosqo cathedral, with the separate bodies of Quesintu and Umantu[16] carved to either side of the front gate, he told the story of how he became a shaman.

'I was sitting in the main square in Qosqo when an old man asked me the time. *9.30*, I replied, then realised he could have looked up to the cathedral clock. 'I would like to work with you,' he smiled. I told him I didn't work for other people, nor did I have any work to give him. 'I'll wait for you on Saturday at my house in Ollantaytambo,' he said.

'That Saturday, I awoke thoughtful and happy. My wife asked me where I was going and when I answered she asked me why. 'I don't know!' I replied. I took the bus to Urumbamba, and from there the little bus to Ollantaytambo. When I arrived I did not know where to go. In fact, I didn't even know the man's name or address. Maybe he was waiting for me in the terminal, I thought, and gave him fifteen minutes.

When he still didn't show, I thought I might as well visit the temple. However, it had too many steps so I turned back. Just then, a truck caught my eye, and following its

Above: Qosqo with Ausengate mountain in the distance

progress I found myself looking towards the next part of town, which was unfamiliar to me. After three blocks, I turned left and a man said, 'I've been waiting for you for a long time, and now I need to work. It's your turn to wait for me.' 'Okay,' I replied and together we entered his house.

'Many people were waiting for healings from him. After three hours, I was tired and gave a yawn. He looked at me and said, 'First lesson, you need to learn patience. Wait. In a short while I will be finished.' Forty-five minutes later he washed his hands and spoke to me. 'This is my work. Would you like to be my student?' 'Oh master,' I replied, 'in Qosqo I am Pepino the Clown and I have my own TV programme. People won't trust me as a healer.' 'First you need to trust yourself. A smile heals the spirit and the self, it is true – if you like, I will teach you about healing bodies.' I nodded in assent and said nothing. That day I started my learning with Don Petro Huaman Quispe. After this meeting, I worked and learned with my master for ten years. He died at ninety-nine years of age on 22nd December 1999.'

That evening Vera undertook a dolphin healing with me. It was kind of her. Afterwards she spoke with Apu and told him she believed I was nearly ready to move to the next level.

On Christmas Day, our party was joined by Louise, an old school friend newly arrived from England to research Waldorf schools in Peru. A kindergarten teacher and feminist on a mission to help children reconnect with land spirits and elementals, she was passionate about earth energies and ceremonies. She was also full of her life in England, both good and bad. Apu had agreed with me that we should postpone our third *ch'ama* ceremony so Louise could join us. Vera, Louise and I spent Christmas together, eating at a restaurant called Jacks, a famous meeting spot amongst Western tourists and travellers. I got the cheque. It seemed an appropriate seasonal gesture. Louise ended up staying with Apu and myself for a fortnight, and the three of us did my third *ch'ama* ceremony as a group. For four or five days we ate together, spent the days with Apu and slept in the same hotel.

The next day, we all visited Tipon, an important temple where the Incas worshipped the water Gods. The 240 hectare site is twenty-three miles south of Qosqo and up in the Gods at 3,530 metres above sea level. It was built in the 1400s by Wiracocha for his aging father, the seventh Inca king. Its Quechuan name is T'inpuq meaning 'where the water boils.' The site has a magnificent irrigation system with fertile terraces, carved stone and complex hydraulic engineering channels which carry the river over nearly vertical drops. The king's servants built terraces to experiment with seed growing – different varieties of corn, potatoes and quinoa.

Vera, Louise and I followed Apu up the steep terraces to the site where the royal family were said to have had their dwellings. As we walked, the sound of water

Above: Tipon – Inca water irrigation system

followed us, engendering a palpable closeness to the Gods. The water of the ceremonial aqueduct flowed between two platforms which represented duality. The fourteen Inca kings, divided into two groups (seven in the upper part of Qosqo and seven in the lower) were built into the layers of the fountain along with representations of the sun and moon and the four regions of the Inca empire. We climbed higher and the three of us and the taxi driver lay in the grasses meditating whilst Apu took to the hills to forage.

As the days passed, Vera increasingly reminded me of my father's sister. After my mother and father separated, she swiftly moved into our farmhouse. Suddenly, I was not able to speak to him without his sister present. Money became a constant difficulty. My old friend from the local primary school – and her daughter – moved into our house with her mother, while I was asked to move out at 16. She stuck to me like glue, joining me on horse rides and accompanying me on dates with my boyfriend. It turned out to be the start of a difficult period lasting until I was 21. My relationship with my father continued to be dominated by others until he passed away.

Apu did little to appease my discomfort. He believed Vera was a message for me. 'It's the cosmos telling you what to do – contacting the shaman within.' Inactivity on his part was part of the teaching strategy. I felt sorely challenged. Everything on my pilgrimage from the language we spoke (now Spanish, no longer Pigeon English) to our route was being determined by others. I felt unseen, and as if I was from a different culture. Vera and Louise translated the conversation and suggested good places to go. The chatter was constant. Words seemed loud but carried no force. There was no time to think, no stillness or presence. My dad's posthumous request was never discussed.

Life was acting as a mirror to my emotions. What I was saying and noticing about others (even inanimate objects such as buildings) reflected what I believed of myself. As daily scenarios played out, I was confronted with unresolved issues about power and control. So it was that in Qosqo, both my behaviour and mental attitude regressed as I struggled to resolve old family issues. At times I was perplexed. At others I felt selfish, immature and stripped naked. I wondered if I had taken on too much and should return home.

The following day, we travelled to the Temple of the Moon at Killarumiyoq for our third *ch'ama* ceremony, stopping off at local markets to buy offerings. The temple has only recently been rediscovered and holds a lot of 'old' energy, perhaps suggesting it is pre-Incan. The site contains numerous vulva-like openings and a beautiful waterfall. During the full moon it is said to shine like quartz and become an inter-dimensional doorway allowing people to connect with Paititi, the etheric city.
The third *ch'ama*, or solar plexus *chakra*, is related to life and the connection we have with *Taita Inti* (Father Sun). This *ch'ama* focuses on opposites – yin and yang, black

Above: Hugging the solar plexus ch'ama despacho

and white, light and dark, masculine and feminine. It enables clear thinking and helps us realise who we are and what we want to be. When it is functioning well we take responsibility for being active players in our own lives. As a group we hoped to balance these energies within us and resolve any long-term issues.

In preparation for the third *ch'ama* ceremony, we sat and meditated in each of the stone windows lining the ceremonial site. At the first window, the magnificent waterfall reminded me of horse-riding in Wales as a young girl. At the second, I recalled Milla Milla falls on the Atherton Tablelands of Australia. In Andean cosmology, windows symbolise the portal through which one gains access to the world of the unknown. They also represent the sacred receptacles with which, by means of light from the sun, the external world (*Hanan Pacha*) communes with the interior (*Ukhu Pacha*) in the cycle that activates the principles of generation that give life to the Earth or our body (*Kay Pacha*).

After a while, Apu called us from our meditations and the four of us sat in a circle. He led our *despacho* ceremony whilst the other two sat either side of him to help. At one point Apu held my eyes in a long searching gaze, across the growing *despacho* offering, his soft brown eyes darting across my blue ones, gathering information and reading my soul. He touched me on a deep level and I started to journey.

I arrived at the back garden of my childhood home, a Somerset farmhouse, climbed into the old gnarled apple tree and like Alice in Wonderland, gently slid into another state of consciousness. I sat on a miniature jewel-encrusted brass bed. It was as if I was downloading new information as I fell slowly into a void. As I travelled downwards, thousands of small coins and bank notes of all denominations, a blank Will and a redundant insurance policy flew along with me. I felt powerless to move away from them.

Suddenly I reached the bottom with a bump. Here the flesh and feathers of the birds in the sky appeared to be burnt off so they became flying skeletons. A bride and groom walked hand in hand far off in the distance. In no time they grew closer then appeared right by my side. The woman carried a marriage licence in her hands. Her body became transparent and I could sense a small area of darkness.

As I returned to reality a bigger picture emerged. Absorbing the energies, there was a deep knowing about how we connect together and the games the Gods play. After the flower and fruit offerings we gave our sacred *despacho* bundle to a waterfall close by. Again the omens blessed us beautifully — a hummingbird appeared, sun breaking through cloud as Vera sang her dolphin song. As we finished our ceremony, a married couple walked over the hills in their wedding outfits seeking a blessing.

When we visited Tambomachay, the Spring of the Quinuapuquio and Puca Pacara, a fortress dedicated to the wind, Vera was with us again. The ever-present guests reminded me of an equine-facilitated learning exercise in Hook, in Hampshire. The horses understood my age-old need to resolve this kind of dilemma, my lack of assertiveness and ability to stand up for myself. 'What were you just thinking?' asked Leanna the facilitator. 'Your horse, Jubilee, agrees — he's licking his lips and chewing.' My answering from the heart often meant that I did not reveal the true meaning or underlying complexity of what I was trying to say, even if people might want to hear it.

Leanna continued: 'Do you see how two female horses, Blessing and Angel, have come to investigate?' Within the next few minutes the youngest of the pair had nuzzled my formation of poles and caused them to fall in a heap. They had been staked into the ground to form a pyramid, with outlying poles aligning the simple central structure to the sun. Now they fell in a triangle, representing a path of consciousness which was in alignment with the natural order, rather than forced.

I reached out to grab the central pole and stop it from joining the others but it was too late. 'Did you anticipate your structure collapsing due to the horse's inquisitiveness?' Leanna asked me. 'Do the random poles on the ground mean anything to you? Do you want to do anything with them now?'

The facilitator turned to the group members one by one, and asked for feedback. One suggested the central pole represented me and the other poles my supports. 'As the poles are leaning on her and not central to her stability, it indicates she is quite capable of standing alone.' Another focused on the young filly smelling dung, surmising I was best left alone to process.

Then Leanna asked, 'What does the young filly represent to you, Jenny?' I replied that my creation was merely a curiosity to her and as I was too slow off the mark to push her away my work got casually undone. 'And the older Shire?' I saw her role as assertively pushing the filly, her nudging merely a desire to learn more about my plans.

Finally Jubilee and I walked back down the paddock and we ended up a few feet from where I had first found him. He had come with me, explored my world and then ultimately returned us both to his. He was well-known for his mastery of dominance games. A nuzzle here, a smile there – all judged to get one over on you and for him to become the leader.

After the *ch'ama* ceremony, I was overwhelmed and visibly distressed at the company. Apu intervened and asked what I wanted. I requested that Vera should only join us if she contributed financially. At the very least an offer of help, perhaps towards the cost of lunch or the taxi. By this stage I was desperate for everyone to go away and leave me alone. I felt bullied by the constant requests to join in. My naivety and kind nature were being taken advantage of. Vera then disappeared. She had befriended another shaman and received an invite to his home.

After this, Louise and I visited Qenqo, one of the largest *wak'as* (holy places) in the Qosqo Region. Its stair design represents space and time. Apu explained that the first step related to the world in which we live and which it is possible to transcend (*Kay Pacha*). The second step represents the world which dreams or the dead give us passage to (*Ukhu Pacha*). The third step concerns the upper world (*Hanan Pacha*) and is associated with the cosmos, eternity, the infinite and the idea of God. At this site, *Kay Pacha* (this world) is represented by a toad, considered to be the announcer and propitiator of rains, linked to natural disasters provoked by excess or lack of water. An interior passage (*Ukhu Pacha*) leads to a funerary altar and the world of the dead. The part of the site corresponding to the *Hanan Pacha* is concerned with the study of cosmic phenomena. An oracle, a tadpole carved in the rocks, forecasts favourable and unfavourable events.

Sacsayhuaman ('Sexy Woman') the head of the Puma city, is where the city's guardian spirits live in a colossal altar to Nature and man's religious spirit. Many of the blocks used to construct the walls are in the shape of people, animals and plants. There is a legendary labyrinth, the Laberintos Cinkanas, under *Sacsayhuaman* allowing travel underground from Puno to Qosqo. One entry point is reportedly at the Sun Island in Bolivia whilst there are others in Puno.

We had not been at this sacred site long when Vera re-appeared in flowing garments.

Above: Doorway at Sacsayhuaman

Arrangements had already been made, I discovered. She greeted Apu warmly and stuck close by him. Afterwards, the three of us underwent healings at the nearby Moon Temple. Apu took us individually underground and in the dark cavern, on a cold slab beneath a chimney opening to the sky, we closed our eyes whilst he weaved his magic above our supine bodies.

A cave is a powerful healer. The womblike space with its stone altar, oppressive, low walls and tunnel-like light above my head seemed to crave my distress and in so doing to invite a rebirth.[17] The cave must have had a big meal that day. Outside again I sat

Above: A cave near the grounds of the Moon Temple

in a meditation. Around me the light was intense and the very rocks I sat on seemed to glow and the grass sparkle. Refreshed, I gazed at this new world in wonder.

On day nine, Apu, Louise and our favourite taxi driver spent time in the sacred valley. Vera had not replied to Apu's email suggesting that if she joined us she might like to contribute. Louise was invited to choose our itinerary. My only request was that we visit Ollantaytambo, where I had previously felt the presence of my father. On the way we passed Pisac where I had had my reading with the Psychic, Joanna. There, the head and wings of a condor

Above: Window to the other Worlds at Ollantaytambo

are carved into the mountain rock in the act of carrying spirit ancestors on its wings. This mythic scavenger has a wingspan of more than 3 metres, allowing it to reach over 6,000 metres in flight. It lives in the craggy cliffs of the highest mountains where the Apus or guardian spirits are said to dwell. In ancient times it was believed to carry the spirits of the dead to the world beyond.

Ollantaytambo is in the Sacred Valley, with its window to the other worlds. The messenger of Wiracocha is represented on a rocky outcrop carrying a pilgrim's bundle on his back to help with the production, storage and redistribution of food. Ollantaytambo itself is a complex (a temple and town) forming a gigantic representation of the Sacred Tree. From Ollantaytambo it is possible to take the train to Machu Picchu, whose sacred geometry was designed here: a temple surrounded by an enormous serpent (the Vilcanota River) winding around the peaks of Machupicchu and Waynapicchu.

Apu and Louise chatted away happily in Spanish whilst I trailed behind. At the gates to the sacred site we stopped to have our photographs taken with an Inca and then commenced Apu's guided tour. First we visited a sacred spring running through the landscape along stone channels and emerging at a small, manmade waterfall. Apu encouraged us to taste the water, smell the air and engage with our senses. We pressed on away from the high stone terraces, making our way along the water course where I had sensed my dad. I tried to engage Apu's attention but he and Louise had other

This page: Terraces at Moray

plans. He was keen for her to scramble up some mountain steps to a rocky shelf, lie there and feel the energies. It was all part of her healing. Once *in situ* he then climbed up and joined her. When he was finished they came down quickly in case a guard appeared. I had been tasked with taking photographs of Louise's healing.

We came over the mountains to Moray and its concentric circular systems for crop development six hundred metres above the valley floor in the red, semi-arid saline plains of Maras. By this time I was distressed and keen to return to Qosqo. What I hadn't been told about was a plan to divert to a location in northern Peru for a further healing for Louise. This would take us three days off our pilgrimage route. Initially, I gave my blessing and suggested I meet Apu later in Huaraz. I was desperate for time alone to integrate my pilgrimage experiences. However, Louise was not comfortable travelling without female company.

On New Year's Eve, Louise and I met up with mutual friends for a spectacular fireworks display at Qosqo cathedral. It was unforgettable, with the noise and lights bouncing off the surrounding hillsides. We were cocooned in the bowl of Qosqo, at its very heart. The next day Louise invited me to her 13th Munai Ki, a healing ceremony for women, at the Moon Temple, near *Sacsayhuaman*.

It was 2nd January when we flew to Lima and took the overnight bus to Churin. Louise, having worked with Apu in Qosqo, had requested a personal treatment and we were *en route* to a location renowned for fertility healing. So it was that we headed for Churin with its spectacular waterfalls, hot springs and mineral spa. At her request, I played chaperone. The route ran along gravel roads passing inches from steep ravines and wild water. Twenty-four hours in all, including the bus breaking down. I didn't manage the trip well.

Eventually, Apu said to me, 'Look in the mirror. You seem to be two different people. Has that always been the case? You are stuck in your own head.' Vera was politely confronted about her financial plans to accompany us further on day trips but I couldn't bring myself to attend that conversation. Part of my energy was still trapped back in my past as a gullible teenager. As Apu spoke these strong words, I looked back and my perspective changed. Vera did not seem so powerful now.

Unfortunately Louise then overheard a private conversation with Apu. I asked if he had invited her to attend the next *ch'ama* with us. This caused major issues and upset and it was made clear to her that I saw the next *ch'ama* as one I would attend with Apu alone. Suddenly, Louise looked vulnerable, like a little girl. I began to lose my fear and feel sympathy towards her. It seemed as if I could absorb the strong, heavy energy around us and embrace some of my own darkness. Apu was nonchalant and appeared completely undisturbed by these goings on. Louise asked if she had overstayed her welcome. 'No,' I said kindly, 'everything is as it should be.'

After Churin, Apu and I travelled on to Huaraz via the Callejón de Huaylas, and on into Chavin de Huantar. We stayed at the Angel hostel just off the main street. It was a disturbed night, my bank cards refusing to work, unlike my insides. Apu seemed unbalanced and disharmonious. He was nursing a cold, complained the taxis were overcharging and the restaurant service slow, and walked on an injured foot. His world was as out of balance as my own. He left shoes and clothing behind him as he travelled in an attempt to discard the heavy energy now trapped inside them. This kind of burden comes with the territory of being an 'empath.'[18]

Ch'ama 4 - A Bridge
Chavin de Huantar, Huaraz, Northern Peru

The fourth ch'ama corresponds with the heart chakra, the thymus gland responsible for the immune system, touch and issues of grief, the ability to fall in love, forgiveness, empathy, unconditional love and an attitude of hope.

That first morning in Huaraz, I woke to find Apu busy removing the blocks from around my heart. Afterwards he said, 'The crown *chakra* is most important for you. If we can get that into equilibrium, maybe you will become an even better shaman than me.' I was surprised until he clarified: 'You have one very important advantage – you're a woman.'

To do this I would need to connect to the energies of *Pachamama*. Augustine, a Pampa Misayok, describes the feeling of connection with the heart, or spiritual ascent, as 'a masculine spirit come into my heart, like my heart opening with the call of *Hampoi* (Welcome) the same way my heart opens when thinking of someone I love.' He continues, 'Then I blow this happiness into your head, your heart and finally your hands.'[19] Augustine calls on different mountains for various purposes – Ausengate for love, the Serpentine for health and Machu Picchu for wealth.

The job of the heart is to integrate our experiences, balance us and to bring us a sense of wholeness. At Chavin de Huantar, the central point of our pilgrimage and heart *ch'ama*, I hoped to radiate outwards and bring love and compassion to everything in my field. To extend beyond myself to embrace a wider web of relationships. In order to truly embrace the energies of the heart we need self-acceptance, to live life without fear, see the world in unity and surrender to forces larger than ourselves. Then there are no boundaries. With this comes a deep sense of peace.

Huaraz, in the heart of the Callejon de Conchucos, is located between the White and Black mountain ranges in the department of Ancash. The area is home to 30 snow-capped peaks, the highest being Mount Huascaran. It is also home to the Chinancocha and Orconcocha lagoons with their intense turquoise water, and to Chavin which is known as the Mother Civilization of the Andes and whose name relates to an archaeological period, a style of art and a hypothetical empire.

The central point of Chavin is the Lanzón, found underground in the main temple in a maze of tunnels where one is able to connect with everything that is in one's heart. Glastonbury, just down the road from my birthplace, is Chavin's masculine counterpart and considered to represent the heart *chakra*. Known as 'the cauldron of the dead,' priestesses dealt there with life, death and rebirth whilst their masculine counterparts lived and worked on the Isle of Anglesey in North Wales. Locals know Glastonbury as a mirror where your reflection shines back at you. It's a place engendering love or hate, happiness or sadness, friendship or enmity.

Geographically, the site is a tor (hill), once an island amid a series of lakes reaching to the coast. Chavin, by contrast, is a bowl or dip surrounded by many mountains in the Andes, seven of them in the shape of a pyramid, stretching vertically up the Americas. The physical structure of the *ch'ama* is the reverse of its opposing *chakra*, vulva-shaped rather than phallic, hills surrounding a sacred site rather than a hill surrounded by flat land. The Lanzón rises from deep in the *Pachamama*, whilst the Glastonbury labyrinth spirals up the tor to give views of the surrounding countryside.

Travelling around the Huaraz area on a tourist bus, Apu and I visited Yungay, scene of the May 1970 earthquake and avalanche where many died and a visiting clown had led three hundred children to safety. This sudden catastrophe was imprinted in the

Above: City of Huaraz

landscape above and below, a landscape cataloguing loss. It was like an astral prison holding tortured souls. The area literally sent shock waves through my body.

We climbed past the cemetery to the white figure of Jesus, arms outstretched over the valley: ruins, relics, barren fields; ceremonial objects where houses used to stand, church stones and above them the cemetery whose higher terraces had survived that dark day. Apu felt the confusion of the buried people and objects in Yungay and promised to enter into an altered state of consciousness to communicate with the trapped souls there and set them free.[20]

On the bus I talked to Apu. I was aware that the fourth *ch'ama* was the point of our spiritual ascent where we could leave the earthly for the divine and was excited at the possibility of connecting with the spirits. I told him a *panchitta* (tarantula) was up in the lodge rafters during my *Ayahuasca* ceremony — which was accompanied by candlelight, sacred cigarette smoke and praying into the hours of darkness. I entered a world of multi-coloured jewels (butterflies, fish, parrots, dolphins) altering in tune with the shaman's singing, whistling, melodic chanting and deep intakes of breath. Radiant, three-dimensional colours cascaded around me. Yet this was but a prologue to the visionary experience. He nodded and gently indicated there was no need to overdo the *Ayahuasca* experience.

The same day we travelled by bus 25 kilometres north-east and up the mountain to the Llanganuku Lakes. These are situated in the Cordillera Blanca, a part of Huascarán National Park. Chinanqucha, 'Lake of the Female,' lies at an altitude of 3,850 metres (12,631 feet) and covers an area of 0.548 kilometres. Urqunqucha, 'Lake of the Male,' lies about 1 kilometre away from Chinanqucha at the end of the Llanganuku valley. The tale goes that the lovers Huandoy and Huascaran were separated by their families and, like the two mountains, destined to be apart forever. I did not understand what the tale of the two young lovers meant. Was something in need of healing or discordant in this environment? Did these ancient people recognise that the structure and consciousness of these two mountains was somehow out of balance?

So we talked about matters of the heart. To move from separation into unity required entering into relationship. It is a frightening prospect to lose yourself in another. Apu talked to me about a *sacred marriage* or *Yanantin* which is a corporeal symmetry of higher and lower, right and left, masculine and feminine. True relationship requires an affinity which is a pulsing together or vibrational quality like the tones of a scale in harmonic resonance.

Apu and I wandered off the beaten track and through prickly scrubland to look at the mountains for signs of life and messages in the rock. We spotted what looked like a cave and a rock shaped like a fox high up in the mountain. Apu explained that in Andean philosophy, the snake and frog, puma and fox and condor and hummingbird were considered complementary opposites. The hummingbird was present for us in our travels from Argentina northwards and carried an important message about flexibility, a need for emotional sweetness and open expressions of love. Foxes on the other hand represent the ability to blend in with your surroundings, remain in the background and trust your senses and intuition. The puma, its opposite in the Andean tradition, is associated with the sun, personal power and courage. I was starting to hear *Pachamama* talk.

These wild animals were comfortable in themselves. They were tuned into their core and the rhythm of the world around them. Each was aware of its characteristics and content being a fox say, as opposed to a puma. Together as complementary opposites, like masculine and feminine, they had a dynamic equilibrium.

On 6th January, Apu and I set off on a tourist bus to Chavin, 109 kilometres from Huaraz, for our heart *ch'ama* ceremony. Chavin was a ceremonial and pilgrimage centre for the Andean religious world and hosted people from as far away as the northern, central and southern coasts, the northern highlands and high jungle of Peru. Their art was intentionally difficult to interpret and only intended to be read by high priests of the Chavin cult. In Chavin there are three important artifacts; the Tello Obelisk, the Tenon heads, and the Lanzón. The Tello Obelisk features images of plants and animals and is thought to portray a creation story whilst the Tenon heads are massive stone carvings of fanged jaguar heads. The Lanzón is a 4.53 metre-long granite shaft carved with an image of a fanged deity.

Our fourth ceremony was to be dedicated to my late father, Peter. Apu seemed happy to enter a trance and allow Dad's spirit to merge with his and become a mouthpiece for the divine. Dad had experienced a dramatic level of loss and Apu proposed entering the 'field of knowing' to unravel the psychic imprint on him and us, his subsequent generations.[21] Remembered for his love of farming, shooting pheasants, a rubber of bridge and a good glass or two of Johnny Walker Black Label, I wanted to make sure he was at rest and his soul transformed.

Still conscious of my lessons in the third *ch'ama* I wondered about my father's role, in particular his commitment to his first family. During the pilgrimage I had become increasingly aware of Apu's resemblance to my father, in particular their physical similarity, the coal black hair and broad-set shoulders. Most uncannily, both had a scar on their face. My dad's, a legacy from a motorbike accident, was a faded part of him by the time I had grown up. Apu's was also an integral part of his story. He had been struck by lightning[22] three times, first on his foot, then at age twenty-one, on his face and finally by his encounter with his master whose name itself meant 'lightning bolt.'

After dad passed, I visited a Glastonbury psychic. Sat in the dark, incense-filled room she whispered to me, 'Someone is here, he has come to say he's sorry.' She described

This page: Preparing our fourth ch'ama ceremony in the main plaza at Chavín

a man with knee and chest problems. It was my Dad. 'Who was with him when he died? I see you, but there are two empty chairs.' His mum was there throughout, helping him.

She continued, 'Do you know a Jack or John?' 'Could Jack be an animal?' I asked. 'He's there, and George who died in a caravan fire. I see a pint of cider. Who is Bill or William? They are both there with a little lady, a delightful woman, maybe an aunt of theirs. Was your dad a farmer? I have a feeling of 'nature' around him. He was not there emotionally and wishes he had done things differently. Dad gives everyone his love.

'Who likes fishing? Who is having a celebration?'

'Oh,' I said, 'I think that would be my brother Tim's 50th.'

'Well, I can see them all up there with their party hats on, glasses in hand waiting to celebrate. They are clapping upstairs.'

My Dad sometimes spent the late afternoons in the Royal Oak. It was a working man's pub. Pickled eggs and beer rather than women that lunch and gourmet food. The main entrance was a concrete walkway with a door off to the right leading into the long wooden serving bar, lino flooring and some old tables and chairs sitting in the corner. Dad and his gang usually sat further along under the window. They played cribbage as a pastime, laughing and swapping stories of the pheasants they had reared and shot. Driving around in their filthy four-wheel drives filled with dog hair and stinking of farm animals, they watched the weather religiously and observed the timing of natural signs like birds nesting and rabbits mating.

Dad's favourite party trick was lifting a ½ hundredweight in each hand and clapping them together in front of his chest. There was a painting of a naked lady in the drinks cupboard one visitor took offence to, and on raucous occasions local farmers came to join the family dinner-table, tucking into pudding or cheese and taking long draughts from their whiskey glasses as they talked. They arrived in good heart then weaved their way through the back door some hours later after a deal had been struck.

Dad's life began to tumble downhill after his stroke. The shell around him cracked, he mellowed a little and he began to voice his emotions. At times he seemed swamped; depressed and more vulnerable.

In his prime Dad was a JP — justice of the peace — sat on the bench in Somerton and Yeovil. One day, I went to watch a case. Three or four local lads sat forlornly at the front. One by one they stood before a row of fusty dignitaries waiting for justice to be handed down. I was mesmerised. Occasionally, mum talks of the husband she left because he was unable to communicate or show emotion to her or to us. Sometimes

This page: Laying our despacho on a sacred stone

Above: *Offering our despacho to the Gods*

she felt she raised the five of us children single-handedly. She says he never talked about the motorbike accident in which a close friend died. He took that family secret to his grave.

During a travel break at Laq Querococha, Apu chatted to our tour guide explaining who we were and what we were doing. As a result, she invited her group to join our ceremony. The bus was full of mixed nationality tourists, mostly Spanish speakers, who gasped in awe to be travelling with a shaman. Apu spent several hours with them, patiently explaining Andean philosophy and undertaking healings and cleansings at Chavin itself.

Unusually, we were unprepared for our ceremony and I hiked the short way into the village in search of alcohol and flowers. Flowers play an important role in most rites of passage – birthdays, coming of age ceremonies, marriages and funerals, as well as recovery from illness. Unfortunately, my lack of Spanish let me down as I tried to buy some alcohol for the ceremony. Meanwhile Apu was having difficulty with officials about getting permission to conduct a formal ceremony.

As we walked towards the centre of the sacred site, Apu gave surreptitious offerings to *Pachamama*. Meanwhile strange things were happening to me. In a walking meditation, and under the guidance of an ostrich[23] with liquid eyes and long eyelashes, I regressed to another life time. At first I was only aware or a heavy weight over my heart and then a man came into view.

He was dressed as an influential Roman soldier in golden sandals, a white silk tunic and gold pleated skirt, breast plate and golden arm bands and gaiters. He wore a helmet with plumage on his head. A very young, fit man stood alone, high up on a vast rocky outcrop. A critical decision had to be made, concerning war tactics. The weather was very hot and dry.

Whilst he meditated he had an awareness of the flapping of bird wings and a pressure on his left arm. The bird landed and pierced his eyes with hers, then cocked her beautiful head to one side as if asking for food. The soldier admired the familiar brown and cream speckled front and distinct colouration of its plumage. 'My falcon,' he thought to himself. He produced a hood out of his pocket and both hawk and warrior stilled as he unravelled the message tied to its leg. The small piece of parchment told him his beloved wife was dead. He should have stayed with her. His heart became gripped with grief.

Then the Roman soldier in his youth and despair led the army forward to a gory end. When captured, he was staked spread-eagled on the ground with a tight garrotte around his neck, so he couldn't attract attention or shout out for help. There the birds pecked out his eyes and in due course his heart was taken, as he was slowly and painfully eaten alive.

Out of the void and mayhem that was once the man's body came a sense of peace. In due course the birds gave back the eyes, replacing them gently in each socket. The garrotte nailed to the back of his neck rotted and loosened so it could be prised off, leaving nothing but a red circular welt. His body rose from its shackles, joined back together and once more assumed the physique of a healthy, young male. Internally his senses reconnected with the mighty engine and loving compassion of his heart.

Then my ostrich guide spoke to me forgiving my far-distant decision which had led to the total destruction of many worthy soldiers. I was reminded of the Pizac journey woman. She had envisioned a bridegroom dressed in white fur carrying his dead wife. She was still in her white wedding gown, decorated in pearls. Grief-stricken and guilty, his betrayal had led to her death. Had I been that bridegroom?

Our first sight of the main temple was against a backdrop of majestic mountains. Steps led down from all sides. Behind and below the temple lies a network of underground corridors used by the priests to prepare for ceremonies. Apu sat cross legged on the ground at the Circular Plaza, a ritually important open-air space serving as an atrium for entering the main temple. Quietly, he constructed our *despacho* and offered cola and water to *Pachamama* whilst our guide talked.

As our group walked on, Apu offered up our *despacho* to the ceremonial spaces and the main temple, a massive flat-topped pyramid. Our destination was the old temple and the Lanzón Gallery, located at the very centre. We passed an enormous ceremonial stone slab, some altar columns and carvings of snakes in the huge white granite and black limestone blocks before reaching the passageways built around a circular courtyard. Our guide gave explanations in Spanish and called upon Apu to expand on their spiritual importance. The group was captivated.

We descended into the dark, mysterious passageways deep under the old temple. The entrance to the left of the courtyard held the Lanzón. Embedded within the Old Temple the phallic column engraved with coded messages buried deep underground reminded me of an ornately carved Maypole. During the wait we inspected the spectacularly beautiful, mysterious representations of flying lizards (or dragons). Many of Chavin's stone sculptures resemble human faces with feline features. These heads represent the transformation from human to feline, symbolically achieved through the ingestion of hallucinogenic substances. Apu is a San Pedro master – that is, he is like Saint Peter, a master who holds the keys to Heaven and speaks of his ability to 'open the gates' into a world where we may heal, discover our divinity and find our purpose on Earth. In the Jaguar Temple we saw a stone carving of just such a *Huachumero* (a male San Pedro master).[24]

Spanish words floated in the air. It was hot and uncomfortable, and my concentration wandered. I was in Malta with my friend Lizzie back when I had been dumped by my first boyfriend and wanted to undertake a boat tour of the world.

Together, we had the most extraordinary twenty-four hours. Asking for a crew job in Valetta Harbour, frustrated by walking around all the boats getting rejections, we stopped at a bar, where a man overheard us. 'Be at the *Wanderlust* in an hour,' he said. We walked down into the yacht's cabin where he introduced us to a couple of other people. Then I saw a photo of Helen, who had visited our house during my years at Exeter University, on the fridge. Our housemate had sailed on the same yacht!

After I got the crew job we went out to celebrate and found ourselves variously in a speeding car, navigating by torch light and narrowly escaping a knife fight in a town house filled with men. At the height of the frenzy, Lizzie knelt by the side of our bed for hours praying hard. After it all went quiet, we crept out unharmed. Lizzie's prayers had worked. In the small hours we walked downhill and found ourselves at an isolated industrial wharf. Exhausted, we sat and contemplated our options: swim or walk back passing the house.

Just then a huge orange freight ship came out of the mist and docked at our wharf. As it neared we waved in excitement and relief. There was my sister Sue waving from the bridge. I felt elated. The ship was so secure, so high, so safe. And it had my family on board. We drank calming vodkas and tonic and after morning showers went out for lunch together. I had had no way of knowing when my sister and brother-in-law, a ship's captain, might have arrived. Yet they did so in our moment of need.

On the sailing trip, surrounded by the enormity of nature we settled into a daily rhythm of one-man, four hour watches around the clock followed by every sixth day as ship's cook. We lit our cigarettes using a magnifying glass, covered eggs in Vaseline to keep them fresh and occasionally we spotted a dolphin or caught a flying fish. Our Aussie captain navigated by the stars and on calm evenings we listened to *The Cars* and *Jethro Tull*, blared out over the wide ocean into infinity. One day on watch the seas were rhythmic and high with waves of perhaps forty feet. The yacht climbed one side and surfed down the other. Keeping on course was draining work, requiring intense concentration to prevent the main sail from whipping back across the deck. My life to that date played before me like a cine-camera reel. Physically I continued at the helm, mentally I was in an altered state of consciousness.

After the tunnel exploration, Apu was called upon to give healings to the tour group. In the wide open space above the old temple he listened to people's ailments and performed healings. There was a queue. Before we left the site, our *despacho* was ceremonially buried in a

Above: Healing at Chavin

Above: The final resting place for Dad's ceremonial despacho

quiet place with a glorious view. My thoughts were with my father and of healing and love. Maybe he was misunderstood, a man who had tried his best whilst his body was locked into that old motorbike trauma, his soul only really able to express feelings in nature. Apu said, 'Peter was here throughout and left when the final offering was given.' I was delighted to have renewed contact.

The day after our ceremony, on our return trip to Lima, we took the eight-hour overnight bus to the coast. Onboard, Apu looked at me and said, 'I will help you become a Queen.' We were both reflective and happy to be in our own space. Needing a holiday, we spent time by the seaside, mostly sleeping, walking, eating and connecting with ourselves. There was an ease to our days, doing what felt right at the time, taking in the local sights: a lady selling toffee apples, a handsome horse tacked in silver and black waiting patiently for a rider in the hot afternoon sun, local buses grunting uphill like old buffalo. We had a mutual respect for boundaries and the freedom to do as we wished — which meant lying still and recovering for Apu's injured feet, wandering aimlessly for me.

It wasn't all relaxation. Apu worked on me as my father instructed what he should change in my energetic vibration, explaining how to tweak and remove the memories no longer necessary. In my mind's eye I imagined Apu giving a *Karpay* or energetic transfer in which he thought of his highest experience, placed his hands on top of my head and energetically transmitted the experience to me. A kaleidoscope of the most beautiful and peaceful images, one after the other rolling on and on - majestic mountains, wild rivers and gentle forests.

Apu encouraged me to enter a different world and recreate my story, to become just a little more joyous and peaceful and to grieve when my heart bonds were broken. Like a shaman we must sometimes sacrifice our old selves before re-emerging. From that day forward my memories of grief and love have sat more easily. I recall the detail but do not re-experience the trauma. My heart is at peace. Apu had formed an alliance with my dad across the last divide, and changed the rubric of my story. He acted as a bridge to the other world and lifted a veil on this one.

Ch'ama 5 - Getting help
Mocoa, Putumayo, Colombia

The fifth ch'ama corresponds with the throat chakra, the thyroid and parathyroid glands responsible for growth, temperature control and energy production and vocation, humour, integrity, hearing, communication and purification.

My computer died before I reached Colombia whilst Apu's *mochila* (backpack) containing his Andean poncho, our ceremonial offering, his computer, camera, bank card and clothes had been stolen at Bogotá airport. Again his life strangely reflected my difficulties. He patiently explained how healing is holistic – heal the person and their environment is healed – and asked me to consider why I was having so many problems with machines such as my laptop. We visited cheap shops for clothing and a witches market to buy new ceremonial offerings, later joining some singers on a bus across town to Montserrat. As we climbed away from the funicular railway Apu saw a hummingbird in the undergrowth. Walking the streets looking for a replacement backpack, Apu was constantly coughing and clearing his throat. 'It is always like this,' he said, 'my body is preparing for the work in Putumayo.'

Apu works for a low hourly rate and has an underlying expectation that people who can afford it will provide gifts to show appreciation and help him survive. This is a shaman's approach. He gives the example of two men, one with five sols in his pocket and the other with ten. They make a purchase for ten sols and agree to go halves. Thus the man with only five sols gives everything he has and has nothing left, whilst the man with ten sols has money left in his pocket. 'This is like the two of us,' Apu said. By choice, he lives hand to mouth, whilst I have money in the bank. If he ever has too much, he gives some away.[25] By contrast I am inconsistent, hoarding at times and being overly generous at others. When I was shopping and being cautious with my money, Apu said, 'You say no, but you don't mean it.'

On our second day in Bogotá we met up with friends of Apu and the four of us travelled north on the city buses to Lake Guatavita. As usual Apu was hungry and we stopped on the outskirts of the city for *Lechona*, a delicious dish of pork with rice, lots of pepper, beans and crackling and *Tamale* – corn cake, rice, beans, pork, chicken and egg with carrot, pepper and curry flavouring. As we were walking through the

This page: Funicular railway, Bogotá

grounds up the steep hill to the lake's rim, Cristina told me, 'Do you know why I love Apu? I saw him on the Island of the Moon in Bolivia working with two women. I was sick. So I went to him and told him I had something wrong with my lungs, could he help? He did something to me, removed an energy and I felt better. He cured me that day and I have always been so grateful.'

By my side, as I puffed uphill, Cristina talked eloquently about her upbringing. She was proud of her heritage, to be born in this region among these people. Apu explained how we choose where we are born and that location defines us. 'Jenny has chosen to be a Celt from Glastonbury.'

At the crater's side we made an offering of beautiful flowers above the green water. Apu threw them, accompanied by our individual prayers, deep into the abyss. The lake has always been of huge ceremonial importance, with golden offerings honouring the Gods, hence the name – El Dorado. The English and Germans once attempted to drain the water to find the gold, leaving a channel gouged out of the deep crater into the surrounding countryside.

Over dinner, Cristina talked of the stress of living in Colombia, until recently a war-torn country with fear of what was around every corner. It reminded me of Northern Ireland, where I once undertook student disability assessments for the Open University. Years after the Troubles had officially ended, the regional trauma still existed. Students on both sides of the divide told me their stories as I assessed their eligibility for free computers and disability-related equipment. Dyslexia and depression existed against a backdrop of kidnap, rape and reinforced glass. People lived in terror with unimaginable secrets and horrors. It was my ignorance – and the presumption that a native English accent bespoke ignorance – that got me through unscathed even as I worked in notorious hotspots the length and breadth of Northern Ireland. Back at the hotel my stomach was distended and I could not sleep. The food and accounts of war had disturbed me. Apu placed his hand on my head and rubbed it gently. Next thing I knew, I could breathe again.

From Bogotá, alive with noise and bustle, we travelled to the Colombian Caribbean where we booked into the more tranquil South of the city, away from the tourist beaches, old castle and city centre. We wandered the streets of Carthegena with its colonial houses, balconies and climbing flowers, eyeing the chubby Botero paintings in the shop windows. At the Cathedral there was a wedding and Apu jokingly asked me, 'Where will *we* go?' I looked at him quizzically. 'Usually, the man asks first.' 'I am not traditional,' he replied with a smile. We walked on. Later that evening we sat in a square watching the extraordinary gyrations of traditional dancers. They were slim, lithe, beautiful and sexy in their brightly-coloured clothing.

We joined a couple of New York newlyweds travelling across the bay to Playa Blanco and later took a trip to the idyllic Islas del Rosario with its troupe of performing

Above: Islas del Rosario

dolphins. Our boat sped past mangrove swamps and huge freighters at anchor, towards a world of white sands, palm leaf thatch, coral, beach masseurs, reggae music, colourful boats and pina coladas. At one point we joined hordes of people being fed in long lines. I felt overwhelmed and suffocated. Apu said gently, 'This is life. It is not the group's fault.'

The ride back was brilliant. Apu was in a joking mood. On the walk back to the hotel, as we passed by a boat in the lagoon, he was reminded of people living in barges in Amsterdam. When my mother left home she went to live on a boat on the River Avon, I told him. I visited often and loved cuddling up in a bunk by the wood burner or watching wildlife paddle by. 'How many years ago?' he asked. 'You were really very young.'

The blockages and symbolic representations of my difficulties continued. In a Bogotá hotel room the temperature control produced first boiling and then near-freezing water and in our Caribbean hotel not only did the water not run, but the room key and air conditioner did not work. I had difficulties spending and getting money: one day the first three ATMs were out of service. I handed over my dollars to Apu for safekeeping, counting on him to get a good exchange rate. That night, I realised that if I lost him I wouldn't be able to pay for food or a hotel. I was reliant on him and had to demonstrate trust. Equally, my responsibility for the money had gone. It had been years since I had given someone else this power.

At times we struggled with each other. Apu laughed at my difficulties boarding a boat, one leg ungraciously straggled over the prow. That day he stayed in town where he met a woman in the park. They talked and she asked him what line of work he was in. 'I am a shaman,' he replied. In the absence of cards, beans or coca leaves he connected with the fallen leaves of a tree and read her future. Later, he appeared at the hotel pool and asked if I would like company. As we talked, a white feather floated towards him in the swimming pool. I remembered his gift of white feathers at Aramu Muru when we first met. 'Why has this feather come back to me?' he asked. 'I just took it and its friend out of the water.'

In the morning, Apu told me he had dreamt of a woman like a mermaid with a serpent's tail who told him it was time to start a new chapter. Over breakfast he showed me a beautiful *object d'art*, useful for his ceremonies. 'I needed to show love for myself,' he said. 'You need to love yourself too, Jenny. Something happened with your father and your experiences in life. You don't love yourself enough. I don't have a problem with your body. That is your problem.'

He continued, 'You know Spanish words, yet you don't speak. Ask yourself what the block is, why you don't express yourself. Ask your body what it is you don't want to say. Where are the sensations?'

We headed into town to the local markets, walked down crowded back alleys and crossed dirty floods of water on planks, beaded in sweat and oppressed by the constant dampness. At a dime store which stocked every item conceivable we bought tweezers, nail clippers, a cushion cover, golden wings and a hammer. We stopped at gold stores. Apu found a gold chain for his sun-disc medallion, with a small golden anchor hanging off it. I asked if he would treasure it forever. 'Maybe, but if I lose the physical connection with this chain I will give it away.' 'We only have physical objects whilst there is a personal connection with them. Just like when we die we lose our body.' He looked down at the anchor. 'Maybe this is a message? Spiritual people come to me saying they have been sent by the Pleiades. They live in the clouds and need to anchor here on Earth. They have a body and are on Earth, so they have work to do here.'

We took the late flight from Carthegena to Bogotá and caught the midnight bus to Neiva, crossing the Colombian Massif with its snowy peaks, mountains and volcanoes, followed by a bus at first light to San Agustin. This is the source of five major rivers which cross the country in different directions – Patia, Putumayo, Cauca, Caqueta and Magalena. Tired and somewhat grumpy after a night with little sleep we booked into a hostel, ate breakfast and spent the afternoon inside craft shops.

The traditional Colombian restaurant was a visual delight with rows of fruit and vegetables displayed around an open kitchen area. As we sat, Apu's eyes alighted on the macramé shop opposite, where an artisan bent over his work, passionately pulling threads. He was a master of his art. Apu went to greet him and stayed chatting until lunch was served, chorizo followed by grilled chicken and an elaborate meat dish. There were huge quantities of food. Then he declared, 'I go,' left me to pay and headed off down the street visiting each store in turn.

At the basket weaver's he ordered three large hoops to make dream catchers; at another store he bought a white poncho for ceremonial work and at yet another two bean rattles for healing work. Meanwhile I meandered down the other side and after an hour reached an emerald store where I was encouraged inside by the owner. In poor English she showed me beautiful rings and pendants. I noticed a turtle necklace. This animal means wisdom and connection with the ancestors whilst emeralds help connect with the crown *chakra* and develop wisdom and positive thinking. I liked the piece and said I would consult with my friend before buying it. 'The Peruvian?' she asked.

The turtle reminded me of my aboriginal guide. At a development circle in Somerset Maria once told me, 'The spirits are getting cross with you – they think it's time you opened up. You have a guide – an Australian, a traditional man. I see a Tea tree and someone picking leaves, a river with a wide bank going into the sea and the tracks of a train (or road train[26]) going over sacred ground.' She continued, 'There's a turtle in the centre of a shield with lines of small dots coming out – maybe seven lines of dots going to the edge of the shield. *Crocodile Dundee* comes to mind – your guide's like the Aborigine in that movie – the tracker who becomes invisible and disappears. This guide is here to help you look at your work differently and introduce new elements to it. He's an Aboriginal medicine man.'

After our negotiations, the vendor gave Apu two small shards of emerald. Earlier he had promised to send the shop positive energies, and now I had bought their wares the shopkeeper was delighted. We left with huge hugs. We wandered on together, this time returning to the macramé shop. We fell into conversation whilst I built a pile of beautiful objects to buy including a butterfly necklace for my God-daughter. All the time Apu encouraged me to spend money: 'These people have spent time and energy making beautiful things for us. We need to buy from them so they can live, to appreciate their work and share our money. What you give to others the cosmos will replace and more. These people will be happy with the exchange. It is good to be rewarded for their hard work and help them connect with abundance. Spend more. All is good.'

We left the town for the San Agustin statues carved from the local rock. Apu stood in front of one, his arms crossed in front 'in the Lemurian tradition'[27] and at another declared, 'That is the tomb of a shaman, I have been talking to him.' At the small waterfall we spotted a bird eating a butterfly and passed a gardener with a machete. Apu said, 'Maybe I will cut off your head, carry it on my belt and then shrink it when I get home, like the shrunken heads on

Above: San Agustin statue, arms crossed in Lemurian tradition

Above: City of Mocoa

my altar.' His big brown eyes looked me over. As we walked, he sang and made noises at the cockerel and dogs - *cock-a-doodle—do! woof! woof!* — then spontaneously lay on the ground to absorb the energy.

After some hours amongst the stones we headed for Mocoa in Putumayo, about four hours' away, and the *Cascades Hornoyaco* (Pressure Cooker and Final Meeting Place), *Cascades Ojo de Dios* (The Eyes of God) and *Cascades Fin Del Mundo* (The End of the World). This was the site of our fifth *ch'ama* ceremony and the reason for our trip to Columbia. We took the next bus out of San Agustin and travelled first by regular coach, then mini bus. Although it was cramped, Apu managed to sleep for the first three hours then cursed my fidgeting for the rest of the trip!

Our last mode of transport was a taxi — three in the front, including the driver, and three in the back. During the night it poured as I lay awake in our spartan room with its naked light bulb, orange curtains and patterned windows.

Apu vanished about midday — there one minute and gone the next. I searched up and down the street, knocked on our hotel room door and put my head in all the shops — nowhere. I wondered if he had been abducted and held to ransom, or his backpack snatched. Eventually I saw him sauntering towards me along the street. He had been caught short with diarrhoea and run to the hotel. Meanwhile I was suffering from constipation and asked him to help buy medicine from the pharmacy. As we were searching, he told me the joke about a man who hadn't gone to the toilet for fifteen days. A consultation with a Western doctor didn't help so he decided to go to a Chinese Doctor who told him the solution was simple and gave him some medicine. He told the man to take just one pill but he took all of them. You can guess what happened next.

Under a full and unusual super moon we travelled deep into the rainforest for our ceremony. I wore a blue summer dress and sandals and carried our offering bunches of white, yellow and red flowers in my hands. We stopped at the wooden toll house and Apu looked intently at a book of photographs as a woman explained the route. Then we walked up and up for nearly three hours. On the way, my pill worked a treat and it felt like a huge release. Once or twice we stopped for a break and a talk. Apu resembled a donkey as he hauled our ceremonial offerings up the mountain. 'What are you, then, Jenny?' 'A pig,' I replied. 'You know Apu, in English, a female donkey is called a Jenny!'

All the time we were moist and warm, surrounded by native forest. Occasionally we came across a wooden house beside the path. At the first waterfall, we changed into swimwear and took a dip in the icy waters. Twice we nearly had to head back, unsure of the route, but each time someone came to our assistance. At the first waterfall two teenagers led us across the river and at the second we followed a guided group who emerged from the undergrowth before crossing the fast flowing river in the opposite direction. 'The end of the world is close at hand,' the guide said.

It was breathtaking. The waters disappeared over a huge drop into the lands below. Butterflies joined us. 'They are making love,' said Apu. 'Look at them flying in circles together.' First, he lay on the edge of this lunar landscape, pock marked with the seasonal flow of water eroding the rock, and looked down into the deep beyond. Then, dressed in a local poncho with orange stripes and sandals, he performed a simple ceremony connecting with the energies of the place and theatrically threw our flowers into the water. He strolled back from the precipice and announced he had talked with the Indians who lived here, on top of the mountain. No doubt he used an old Andean initiation into the feminine mysteries to invoke their Spirit to enter into him. All the time, I kept away from the edge fearing I would jump off. Apu's brown eyes met mine. 'Today is as good a day as any to die.' His words resounded in my head.

After our ceremony, Apu declared he was going to the bottom of the waterfall and asked if I wanted to accompany him. I declined but felt very alone. He descended along a path of tangled roots with a faded, tatty sign 'Fin de Mondo' hanging above it. Just then, the two teenagers re-appeared, screamed, smiled, pretended to push each

Above: End of the World cascades and site of our throat ch'ama ceremony

other off and then lay above the abyss on top of each other, archetypal young lovers. The girl had pink and green soles and the boy's clothes were like part of a yellow and black wet suit. We communicated by gestures and looks. 'Where is your friend?' they motioned, and I indicated downwards. They balanced on their chests with their heads extending over the precipice, whistled to Apu and waved with both hands. My body was all goose pimples. After a long while, they left with a wave.

Then their two friends appeared. 'Hola!' they called and used pointing and facial expressions to enquire about their friends, promptly disappearing up the ladder after them. I performed a little ceremony and gave our ceremonial wine to feed *Pachamama*. The sound of birds in the trees, the rustle of wind in big green leaves and water rushing off the rocky escarpment captivated me and I absorbed the energies from around me. I felt the blades of green grass high on the banks, the cool, smooth rock between my toes and the beautiful cascading waters leech into me. Each elemental spoke its own language somehow communicating its thoughts.

As my brain stilled, I was entranced into a journey. I felt like a murmuration of starlings. Thousands of migrating birds moving in unison, like the swish of a Gipsy girl's dancing skirts. It was a familiar sight on the Somerset reed beds in mid-Winter. In my hand I carried a pile of books, a meeting agenda and a computer. As the latter whirled and ticked, spewing out a trail of emails, I travelled deeper into the cosmos past Earth and Venus and on into the Milky Way where my perspective changed. I felt a burning desire to return to the void, a complete and perfect emptiness, where there was no sensation or feeling and the only sound was that of my breathing.

Above: Fin del Mundo

Eyes closed, I stepped beyond the edge, effortlessly into the brink of Creation. Here the waters were still and calm. Time stopped. With nothing to do and empty space all around me, my reason for being became clear.

Everything became silent and dusk was drawing in, when a mangy yellow dog emerged and sat opposite me with woeful eyes and a nasty abscess at the base of its tail. He was my friend and left with a stomach full of avocado. I started to feel insecure, damp, cold and alone and put up a silent prayer. Minutes later, as I changed out of my wet clothes Apu reappeared. I had had company for the full two hours he had been away.

Apu offered me a walking stick and, still damp, we hurried down in the failing light. We navigated the rapids getting wet up to our thighs, climbing up ladders and across rocks, and we took a brief skinny dip before I fell on my right buttock in the wet, slimy conditions. I found that if my internal chatter was negative I slipped – so from then on I kept my mind empty. At the top of the mountain, after the waterfalls, we descended past the benches where Apu declared the site of the throat *chakra* portal. Dusk was falling fast and we were lucky to have got down before dark. Muddy, wet and exhausted, we crossed the wooden slatted bridge which swayed from side to side high above the boiling river. Apu threw his stick into the water, thanking it for a job well done. On the main road we flagged down a taxi and sat back under a tarpaulin. We got into town at seven p.m. At the hotel, Apu thanked me for my company on a very special day with the masters. Yet he looked preoccupied.

We were tired and ill-humoured on our return to Bogata. I asked Apu, 'What did you buy?' He retaliated with silence. He was determined to get his point across. 'Why

This page: The route to Cascades Fin del Mundo

do you need to ask me what I buy? Without trust there is no relationship.' At the food stall in the bus station I felt his strong, furious energetic release. The force of it made me cry. Was he using his body like a tuning fork and once again reflecting my emotion? It reminded me of what I had experienced with so many clients over the years. At times the force of their pent-up emotion felt strong enough to knock me clean off my chair. Eventually we booked into a hotel around midnight. We were friends again in the morning. That night, high up above the city we drank cinnamon mixed with alcohol and discovered that Bogotá, high in the Andes, was once a huge lake, like Titicaca, and that the water table was still only a few metres below ground.

On our last day in Bogotá, Apu performed a healing on Cristina at her request, tracking and removing bad energy. He used a sacred pendulum to connect to the energies and seek answers. A small heavy ball made of *Champi*, it was one inch in diameter on a dark red cord about the length of the span of an arm from elbow to extended hand. After the healing, he started to talk. Apu told us he had had troubles on his walk down to the bottom of the waterfall. He had lost his route, slipped twenty metres and thought his end had come. In need of assistance, he shouted *S.O.S!* at the top of his lungs. He looked at me and said, 'This is important. I never ask for help. When I had problems with my heart, when I was involved in a bad car accident in which the driver and passengers died and I was injured, I never asked for help.' He touched the scar on his forehead. 'On the mountain, I opened my throat and begged for assistance.'

Ch'ama 6 - Becoming Whole
Chichen Itza, Merida, Yucatan

The sixth ch'ama corresponds with the third-eye chakra, the pineal gland responsible for promoting sleep, regulating the body clock and supporting libido, also for visions, dreams, learning and clairvoyance.

High up in the clouds, as we travelled towards Mexico, I was in an inquisitive mood and keen to learn more about Apu's work on our pilgrimage. Sat beside me on the flight, he was a captive audience. As he finished a small coughing fit I asked him how he would activate the sixth *ch'ama*. 'First, I will have to connect with it. It is not possible to say what I will do, each time it is different, but it is always important to take an offering to feed *Pachamama* and to communicate our thanks.' He continued, 'Afterwards, I hope my level of wisdom is sufficient to have got clear information about the steps we must both take, and on how to spread the word to those who follow a spiritual path. Perhaps we can do this very soon but I cannot say before finishing all the *ch'ama* work.'

As our meal was served another question occurred to me. How did our ancestors know how to find the *ch'ama* locations, for example Chichen Itza? 'This is a difficult question to answer in words,' he said. 'As I have told you before, in Andean culture, feeling is very important. Our ancestors followed their hearts.' I had read of hidden forces in the landscape and important sacred sites and power places located along Ley lines.[28] Apu looked thoughtful, 'I would have to read what you read before commenting on that. Perhaps I know it in a different way. I have told you things about my tradition. The story of my master and his visit to the doorway at Aramu Muru is a possible response, as well as the etheric cities in each *ch'ama*.'

Apu yawned. I tried my luck once more and mentioned that sacred sites like Stonehenge are thought to act as an earthing circuit or acupuncture point in the land. Did any of the *ch'amas* act in a similar way? 'It is not the same,' he replied. '*Sunkanka*, or standing stones, whether placed or natural, are there to control outbreaks of energy as well as determine the movements of the cosmos. The *ch'amas* are points of accumulation and outbreaks of energy which determine the forces that control *Pachamama*.' He looked at me and wiggled his eyebrows. 'One more question and then I will sleep.' 'Do you believe people control the land or the land controls

This page: Colourful Mexican cloth

Above: Apu feeling the energies

the people?' I asked quickly. 'People who believe that they dominate the Earth are not in a positive vibration and appear to dominate only whilst the Earth allows them to. All these people together do not have the energy to compete with *Pachamama*. We, the spiritual people, are here to balance this.' Apu promptly closed his eyes leaving me to wonder as we neared Chichen Itza whether he was dreaming.

As Apu slept, I mentally reviewed the previous *ch'ama*. The fifth, concerned with expression – communication, vocation or work from the heart, integrity and telling the truth – is thought to have a special connection with the sacral at Lake Titicaca. Apu had said that the power of words can heal or damage depending on how they are delivered. This power is generated by the intention of the being, the person who delivers the words. The lessons of this place would include retrieving my power from false truths and learning to act on my internal direction. To do this I would need to see the truth or symbolic meaning in a situation and let go of my illusions. Let go of long held fears from my shadow side and release negative thoughts towards myself and others.

Even though the rest of our flight to Cancun via Mexico City was uneventful, it was long enough and we arrived tired and disorientated. Both of us were unfamiliar with Mexico and needed to get accustomed to the new energies. Checking into a small *pension* we explored the surrounding town and recovered ourselves a little. The temperature was idyllic on the Mexican Caribbean and even away from the main tourist spots there was plenty to do and see. We enjoyed delicious *Mole*, a Oaxacan dish, and *Coctel de Camaron*, a seafood dish with avocado, shrimps and tomato sauce.

The next day we headed towards Chichen Itza but miscalculated and found our bus pulling up in Merida instead. As we travelled, Apu asked if I was alright. My brother-in-law was due to have an operation and I was worried about him. 'On what part of the body?' he asked. 'A knee replacement.' 'What is his name?' 'Gunnar.' Then he was silent, absent for a matter of seconds. Returning, he said, 'The operation will go well.'

In Merida, there was no high-rise skyline. The streets were laid out in a grid-like system below a cathedral atop an old Mayan site which lays claim to being the oldest in all the Americas. Apu was quite unwell with a bad cough and upset stomach so I left him to the lizards and ceiling fan to explore the town alone. I found myself navigating the streets by banana stalls, a fat man slouched beside his newspaper stand and blasts of loud music. My landscape was one of colour, sound and familiarity. My feet followed the melodic contours of the land as if they were songlines.[29]

Rested, we tracked our way back to Chichen Itza and based ourselves in the small town of Piste, a mile from the sacred site. We found a hotel and then explored the main street, peering into shops and inspecting local wares. In the morning we breakfasted in the small town and talked with the owner of a sandwich bar there. Immediately it became clear we were in a different culture. He made a traditional chicken sandwich and served coffee whilst the man at the adjacent stall sold the same sandwich but with pork, and served tea. On the other side of town, two more men sold the same wares. It is part of the Mayan philosophy to be clear about what you offer and not compete, just as it is to ask for goods rather than money, swapping food for glasses, a hat, perhaps a bag.

Above: Mayan shape-shifter

Having eaten, we set off to Chichen Itza along the dusty roadway. The name is said to derive from the Mayan language, *Chi* — 'mouth,' *Chen* — 'well' and *Itza* — the tribe which inhabited the area. *Itza* might also translate as 'enchantment of the water' (*its* 'sorcerer' and *ha* 'water'). When we arrived, Apu walked with his hands spread facing downwards, feeling the energy, picking up the vibration of the land, celebrating the new and unknown. The atmosphere was palpable and alive with imagery and magic everywhere. I loved the wild cat sounds as we walked, the Mayan sense of colour — particularly the use of pink, yellow and turquoise — the reverence for animals and the barter-based culture.

We hired an English and Spanish speaking guide to explain Chichen Itza's spiritual significance. The main temple, the pyramid of Kukuulkaan, served as a universal solar calendar. At the base of the steep steps, which ascended on all four sides to a square altar housing the three masks of Lord Chaak, our guide explained the calendar. He pointed out some of the complex symbols contained within the pyramidal structure, including its nine levels representing the nine planets of our solar system and the four corners symbolising the seasons. Afterwards, he showed us important texts concerning the Mayan calendar system, and referred to the Popol Vuh, the most important of Mayan scriptures, which depicts the 'World Tree.' This sacred tree is part of the Mayan creation mythology and considered the *axis mundi* of the Earth.

Walking towards the Temple of Warriors, our guide explained that the Mayans used sound to help change vibration,[30] and employed techniques to enhance the third eye, such as extending the head to bring the pituitary and pineal glands closer together. Mention psychedelic drugs, the lotus position and meditation to an

This page: Apu at the Kukulkan Pyramid in Chichen-Itza which is also known as "El Castillo" (the castle)

Above: Apu walking past the Ossuary

ancient Mayan and they would not bat an eyelid. Using calibrated tuning forks, they adjusted any organ frequency which was out of balance and used ritual body posture to induce a shifting of consciousness or 'ecstatic alternate reality' experience. The Mayan civilisation knew how to exploit magnetism to enhance human intelligence, reproduction and healing powers. They emulated the power and qualities of animals, in particular jaguars.

As he talked, I felt more in tune with the environment. It was as if I was almost in another reality. Miraculously I saw a world I had never seen before. Yet at the same time I felt I must have done, hundreds of times, as it had been there all along. We walked on towards the Nunnery and the Observatory through the aisles of stalls with their colourful ethnic trinkets made by indigenous craftsmen, and across the vast plaza in front of the pyramid of Kukuulkaan. In the wilting midday heat we moved onto the Grand Ball Court, where ceremonial games had had a life or death outcome.[31]

Our guide explained the importance of home and environment to the Mayans. They believed that people radiate and absorb energy which affects both the spaces they occupy (landscapes, cities, neighbours, workspaces) and their physical bodies. Every gathering creates a group energy. Energy fields, created by the conscious intent of a group, influence the sense of connection and support. This energy can be used for

Above: Apu kneeling in front of the Pyramid of Kukuulkaan

personal, group or environmental healing or tapped into as a source of inspiration. Apu looked thoughtful. 'Mayans must have had clarity and awareness. When your attention is not focused on thinking, it is focused on your surroundings.'

The next day we returned to Chichen Itza, waving in acknowledgement to the guides at the entrance. Apu stopped to greet our guide from the previous day and explain the importance of our ceremony. Within minutes he had changed into his colourful poncho and hat with woollen pompoms, drawing much attention. As we walked, people watched and took photographs. First Apu made offerings at the four sides of the pyramid of Kukuulkaan and in front of the Temple of Warriors and the Observatory. He dropped his backpack to the bare earth to kneel at each building for long minutes, communing with the distant past.

We then found a raised stone bed in a small grove of trees within which we could conduct our ceremony. Apu was going to invoke the qualities and mysteries of the sixth *ch'ama* to connect with us. My senses were tickled by the sandy, dry smell of the earth. I tasted the hot salty flavour of sweat as it dripped from my brow, down my face and into my mouth. A million vibrant colours waved in the distant breeze and feelings of death and sacrifice emanated from those ancient walls against a backdrop of jaguar roars.

Above: Apu constructed our despacho with prayers and intention

Overwhelmed, I found myself at the head of my ancestral line as it stretched far back in time. Hundreds of dimly perceived men and women dressed in old English garb or the tartans of the Scottish and Irish. Most were standing alone but occasionally, like the great hero twins of the Popol Vuh legend, one had an identical twin by their side. I felt so very tired.

Then my hands enclosed a crystal skull and I gazed deep within. The doorway to another world opened and I was communicating with spirits and ancestors. Mysteriously I began to view happenings back in England. Like a tuned-in radio I became part of the Glastonbury Zodiac.[32] I entered the hill fort at Compton Dundon where I communicated with the fairy people. They told me secrets I had once known when I had lived with them long ago. The plants and the trees talked with me. An owl flew by and gave me wise insights. Up on the promontory, which overlooks the Somerset flatlands, my eyes stretched to locate Etsome Bridge, where I connected with my other half.

The completed *despacho* was a work of art, like a beautiful mandala. We devoted this ceremony to my brother-in-law Gunnar, who was having his knee operation that day, and others who were sick and unwell. In the shade, Apu constructed our *despacho* with prayers and intention. A guard ambled by and after a brief word in Spanish watched on and kept other tourists away. He was honoured to be part of our process. 'Don't sacrifice your wife at the Cenote,' he shouted after us as we left. Hugging the *despacho* package close to my heart, we reached the Sacred Cenote and sat in the sticky heat. There we patiently awaited a quiet time before offering our ceremony to the Earth, above the water's edge.

The hot mile-long walk back into Piste found me completely exhausted. It was difficult to put one foot in front of the other. Lying on my bed unable to move, my feet ached. Disorientated I calmed myself by repacking my rucksack. Later I noticed Apu had copied me and done the same. As I drifted into a deep sleep I reflected on my third eye period, from the age of thirty-five to forty-two. It was a happy time, living in the Australian Snowy mountains and at Yatte Yattah on the coast. I enjoyed my work and made lifelong friends. The period began with a long trip and ended with my return to England. Tired of long-haul flights at that point in my life, I decided to return overland to the United Kingdom.

In China, I witnessed crowded stations and carriages filled to bursting, bras and fur coats peeping from bags, samovars and menus consisting of vodka and kuritsa. Endless card games and stories by Chinese nuclear scientists. Engineers touting their wares at each station. In the small hours one morning, Mongolian guards came through each carriage asking to see visas. A few of us didn't have the right paperwork and had to disembark and stand in a short queue outside an office. The lights burned brightly as four or five officials bent to their work. One collected passports, the next found a blank page, another stamped it and finally the last handed it back. It was cold, bleak and very dark. 'Where are you from?' asked the man next to me. 'Somerset,' I replied, and the next man in line said he was also from Somerset, as did another. On that misty morning it turned out that the five people in that queue all came from Somerset. One had even gone to school with my brother, Tim.

At dinner that evening, the subject of Gunnar, illness and disability came up. I asked whether Apu ever removed weaponry from people – stakes, arrows, daggers in the heart and the like? He really came awake. 'This is important work. Can you do this? Would you like to work together?'

'I would love to,' I replied.

Apu's approach was far removed from my normal job. Most of my life I have worked with people with disabilities. In the early days, my job was to design a training program to help people with spinal injuries get on with their lives and find appropriate work. We achieved this with relish, setting up structured 'independent living' and computer courses, hydroponics farms, musical instrument adaption workshops and Moroccan retreats. We trained all kinds of people – care staff and Qantas employees among them. It was a steep learning curve: dropped mouthpieces, driving slowly so as not to bounce too much, and quietly emptying leg bags in corners. I loved everything about the job.

Afterwards I set off alone up the mountain, to open a new Commonwealth Rehabilitation Service (CRS) office. My manager's parting words were, 'If you ever have a car accident, get out of the car, take out the radio, find a tree and sling the aerial over a branch. Then use the handle to crank-start the radio and call the flying doctor. They'll come and sort you out. We won't be able to do anything much from down here.'

My work territory was 250,000 square kilometres stretching from Weipa in far north Queensland through mining land, then small country towns like Mareeba, Atherton and Ravenshoe and into vast tracts of treeless territory. I departed for my government job, alive with stories of brewing a morning cuppa on your own roadside fire, rowing between client appointments on the Torres Strait Islands and interviewing clients in their 'humpies' – homes built of local materials on a plot of land, with a Billy can over an open fire, bed under a tin roof and a couple of wooden walls for shelter from the elements.

Back in the 90s, the Atherton Tablelands was a place where you wrote your own rule book. Three main groups of people lived up there during my stay: the alternative hippy community, full of love and crystals, redneck farmers who had brought up their families in these isolated spots for years past, and the 'wingers' and 'peg legs' who gravitated to the Far North so they could disappear in name and body, often growing illegal crops outback.

My clients had more than their fair share of amputations, gunshot wounds, psychiatric illness and bad backs from lifting or shearing sheep for hours each day. Back then, it was a wild territory where women dressed in stockings and tiaras went to horse races in sweltering 40 degree heat while druggies fell off their motorbikes, raided each other's crops and indulged in gang warfare.

After our ceremony at Chichen Itza we travelled in the Cancun area, renowned for its white sands and the transparent waters of the Caribbean. The prevalence of local limestone has created a landscape of holes, caverns, sinkholes and cenotes. In Tulum, a trading port, birds and large lizards peeked from the palms and from under the grey rock. The port took an active role in the redistribution of local and foreign products which arrived via sea, river and land from as far away as Central America, the Pacific and Gulf Coasts and Central Mexico.

The site was dedicated to politics, magic-religious rituals and the arts, and astronomical observations – particularly of the planet Venus. There were remnants of columns and ancient windows to other worlds. The facades had originally been painted in bright colours and decorated with sculptures and the altars filled with offerings whose scents filled the air. The site was a fusion of sunrise, midday and sunset; land, sea and sky; religion, politics and trade; the Mayan and the Spanish.

Tulum stands out in my mind for its multi-coloured cloths – deep red, orange, pink, yellow and blue embroidery flapping above the postcards and brick-a-brac, the trees adance with wildlife. As we were walking through the brightly coloured stalls, Apu bent down and picked up four or five screws from beside the pavement. 'We will meet new friends.'

One night, we slept in an incredibly noisy high-street alive with Mexican music. We were surrounded by tourists, men with backpacks, beautiful hippies and local women wearing *ternos* (floral dresses). I dreamed of a horse escaping from a locked stable, then galloping to the top of a hill where it freely chose to live in a field of cows. I was miserable and had caught Apu's Merida bug. That day, much like the majority of my forties, I was unable to speak for myself and out of tune. Indeed, in my crown *chakra* period, things reached a peak when, in a meeting of Government and University teachers in Estonia, I found myself unable to introduce myself or even say my name. This was the time Apu was most concerned about.

Happily, things changed. We went out for breakfast the next morning having slept badly and within minutes a street hawker came past our table selling royal jelly, a wonderful cough remedy.

The last day in the Yucatan Peninsula we visited a cenote and sat on the beach. It was another scorcher and, feeling the financial pinch, we walked from the kiosk instead of taking a car or bus. It was a long walk along a dirt track and blisteringly hot by the time we arrived. After changing into swimwear in the undergrowth, the water was blissful, clear and cool. We swung gently in hammocks, where we were eaten alive by insects, and hitched back to the main road with an English couple before taking a bus up to the beaches. There we found miles of white sand dotted with sun-umbrellas and tourists drinking cocktails. After a dip in the warm sea we wandered round the vast shopping area perpendicular to the beach, buying Mexican sombreros and pretty cloth until it was time to leave.

Walking to the bus, we stopped to look at a lace top in a shop window. Inside, a young man was talking urgently in Spanish to the shopkeeper. First Apu listened intently and then they fell into conversation and moved outside. Nobody else was taking any notice but suddenly two or three people became interested in what the boy had to say. It seemed he and his girlfriend had been robbed in their hotel the previous night, and he needed to sell his mobile phone, their only belonging of value, to get back to their home in Mexico City. Other people appeared at the shop door before discreetly disappearing back inside. At the end of the negotiation the couple departed with a bus ticket back home while Apu was in possession of a cracking phone. Everyone was happy.

Ch'ama 7 - Connecting to Self
Teotihuacan, Mexico

The seventh ch'ama corresponds with the crown chakra, the pituitary gland responsible for hormones and issues of clairsentience, bliss, enlightenment, peace and understanding.

My strongest memory of Pubula is of Apu holding a small baby to his chest at the temple of Tlaxcala, high up a wind-swept hill. The tightly swaddled baby gurgled softly whilst her mother looked on, ecstatic. The assembled crowd, sitting in a rough circle around Apu and the baby, were silent, wishing only the best for this small being. At the completion of the ceremony they applauded loudly and took photographs for posterity. This impromptu blessing at the temple of Tlaxcala set the scene for the seventh *ch'ama*.

Time and again, Apu was asked to connect with previously unknown individuals and groups and to perform ceremonies with them. Occasionally, the requests were simple, at other times elaborate. He always said yes and gave his time and energy freely. Somehow his vocation as a priest and purity of intent shone through, attracting things, people, animals and magical events towards him. I was reminded of a lesson in Africa when a group of us visited school children in a desperately poor area of Lusaka. Our leader was insistent we did away with any bad feelings and greeted the children as equals and people of importance. It was a big occasion for a doctor and white people to visit. She said our contact that day, our willingness to answer questions, our interest in the children's lives and welfare, our good humour and wish to join in, might make a huge difference to their lives. It could be a turning point they would always remember.

On setting foot in Mexico City, we headed for Pubula, where Apu had been invited to perform a ceremony alongside a local shaman. We were exhausted after a a night flight and a subsequent night on the road, only being able to snatch a little sleep on the bus station floor. After settling into our accommodation we wandered up the road to visit our hostess, Bertha, an old friend of Apu's who ran a healing centre.

This page: Apu thanking the Gods with his arms crossed Lemurian-style

I had not met Bertha before, and was intrigued by her talk of a gathering of like-minded people in Egypt. In particular, how they had all entered the fifth dimension, witnessed pyramids turning green, and created the perfect male and female energies.

On the day of the ceremony, a group of some twenty people gathered at the centre and we set off together in a small cavalcade of cars. First, we paid homage at two large stone basins at the base of the ancient pyramid. Then we zigzagged after each other up the steep temple steps into a vast barren, windswept space. At the top we could see the spiral building opposite our ceremonial hill which had once been used as an astronomical observatory or temple to the wind God. A local shaman opened the ceremony by leading the group in each of the four directions and then Apu built our *despacho* offering layer by layer, explaining its purpose as he went along. After blessing each of the group, our offering was buried underground through a grid at the centre of a circle. Then we descended.

Apu and I spent another night in Pubula before heading back to Mexico City via Guadalupe and on to Teotihuacan for our *ch'ama* ceremony. On our first day in the vast city we walked down a broad avenue towards the Basilica of Our Lady of Guadalupe, the most-visited Catholic pilgrimage site and third most-visited sacred site in the world. It was filled with golden-domed churches. We crossed a plaza and had the choice of turning left towards the modern religious building, continuing straight on towards the ornate older churches, or climbing the steps towards Tepeyac Hill.

Up the hill, inside the small church (which was decked with taut pink streamers) we learned the history of Guadalupe. As one of the few stories in the Southern and Central Americas about an Indian encountering the divine, it accounts for the site's enormous popularity amongst the indigenous population. In 1531, a lowly Indian peasant, Juan Diego, saw a vision of a maiden here, who told him to build a church on this site. Upon hearing his story, the archbishop Zumárraga instructed him to return and ask the lady for a miraculous sign to prove her identity. First, the boy's sickly uncle was healed. and then Juan was told to gather flowers from the normally barren hill. He found Castilian roses, not native to Mexico, blooming on a hillside and collected them in his cloak. When he returned to the archbishop and dropped the flowers to the floor, the fabric of his cloak was imprinted with the image of the Virgin.

From Guadalupe we travelled onwards to Teotihuacan — 'where the Gods came down to Earth' — the great Toltec city north of Mexico City. On the way to the great temples of Teotihuacan, men sang on the bus and school children chattered. When we arrived the enormous scale came as a surprise. The site contains hundreds of pyramids with carvings of water serpents and earth monsters. At the temple of Quetzalcoatl

This page: Our Lady of Guadalupe

there are graves of warriors who had been sacrificed as offerings with their hands tied behind their backs. They are wearing ear-spools of green stone, shell beaded necklaces and elaborate bracelets around their upper arms. The Teotihuacans had worshipped gods associated with water, the Earth and fertility including Quetzalcoatl, the Feathered Serpent.[33]

After it fell, Teotihuacan became a place of pilgrimage where people performed ceremonies to honour the gods. According to legend, the site of this ancient city marks the site of the creation of the Fourth Sun which lit the world in which the heirs of the Teotihuacan culture lived. Mayan architectural principles demonstrate how the divine operates in the material realm: just as each number is ruled by a god or divine principle, so is each level of each pyramid. Usually the even-numbered heavens are more nurturing and feminine and the odd-numbered heavens more male and warlike. The first six numbers represent the creation and building of an issue, the seventh a creative explosion and the final six add complexity resulting in a new creation.

We planned to conduct our seventh, and final, feminine *ch'ama* ceremony in the Central American equivalent of what Tibetans refer to as 'the thousand lotus blossom *chakra.*' It represents spiritual ecstasy and heralds our connection with the divine. As with so many before us, we came to link with those energies. Sat under a tree inside the temple grounds in sight of the avenue of the dead, Apu performed a simple but poignant ceremony. It was in honour of Sophie, my mum's dog who had passed away the day before, although Apu's activation of this *ch'ama* was intended for the whole of humanity.

Like Apu in Chichen Itza, I tried to use my hands like divining rods, holding them loosely out in front of my body with my right thumb as a guide. I wanted to see if my hands could give me information about this sacred site and lead me to key monuments and artefacts of archaeological importance. As we walked I honed in on the energies, trying to sense information, to feel the present, past and future of people around me and to retrieve information from near-by buildings. As we passed the clock face of Teotihuacan my mind focussed on the rising and setting of the Pleiades star cluster and the stone skull beneath the Pyramid of the Sun. Could I journey to the holiest of holies - a cave beneath the Sun Pyramid - where people native to this area believed the world was born and look deeply into the skull housed there?[34]

A bee passed by, Zzz, Zzz and I lost myself. I wore a white skull cap that covered my head. As the bee got louder, to my surprise my focus became more intense. I was transported through a time portal to Stonehenge. First I was aware of Apu hitchhiking along the road, then the rooks and jackdaws, guardians of the stones, receiving an offering of bird food. I navigated my way by following old lines gouged deep into the earth and came into the Henge over the circular earthworks, through the Heel stone and under the lintel of the mighty Sarsen main doorway. There was a silver streak of lightning directly above my head then a loud thunder clap. Spiralling five times over the altar, a gust of wind blew my skull cap clean off.

Then I was transported on a shaft of golden light to the archaic Doric colonnade in Gaudi's Park Guell in Barcelona. Thirty holes in my head blew out dense, black smoke and any fear mysteriously left me. I was reborn as a jewel-encrusted baby lain naked under a round, coloured plafond. My body was covered in crystals and gemstones. A golden hair clip lay by my side. My head became full of delicate, perfumed rainbow-coloured flowers. I felt ecstatic, whole and able to love myself.

After the ceremony we walked, *despacho* offering in hand, through the Citadel towards the Temple of the Sun. Apu talked to vendors lining the route, eventually entering into a deep conversation with a lone stall-holder. Then magic happened and a connection was made. This man was offering a visit to the most sacred site in the temple, one not accessible to tourists. We followed him underground and after a nod of approval dropped our ceremonial bundle down a deep, deep well.

All along, Apu had maintained that I needed help to fully open this *chakra*. If I could feel with my heart, manage to not always think in the rational Western way, and stop alternating between a woman and child, I too might experience a deep sense of inner peace. He hoped this *chakra* would help me integrate my whole system from root to crown – to be transformed and radiate love, freed from my human brain and immersed in a greater truth. An opened crown *chakra* might even lead to my becoming a healer.

Instinct told me that control issues lay behind my insistence on thinking and analysing rather than using my intuition. Once again, it was a horse, Joseph, that provided a key. For me he embodied harmony with male energies, unity rather than domination or submission. He encompassed the relationship I had with my childhood pony Jack, whom my parents bought to help me recover from my illness and who set me free. It was a profound connection which included mutual willingness, consideration and lightness of agenda. An ability to follow or be led.

My task that Spring morning was to get Joseph to follow me without touching him. There were two tools I could use: a short rope or a whip. Neither could touch his skin. My initial endeavour resulted in continued munching and a resolute ignoring of my unspoken wishes. Upping the ante by making appealing sounds did little. Even hitting the ground with the whip just in front of his face was largely unsuccessful. Eventually I admitted defeat and requested time out to digest and reconsider. Did I rant and rave? Certainly there was a mixture of guilt and needing to grow up. I hadn't come to terms with my lack of power over Jack's sale and his future home, and imagined him constantly circling an indoor dressage arena in an unknown riding

This page: Apu, with our new friends, walking to the top of the Pyramid of the Sun

stables. With the premature dissolution of our relationship came mistrust and over-analysis. After lunch I was politely asked if I would like another go at getting Joseph to follow me.

I walked purposefully across the paddock. As I neared Joseph, he raised his head, acknowledged me and ambled across. I stopped dead in my tracks, silently said hello, did a little leap for joy and together we returned to the group. Side by side, a one ton shire-horse and his new herd member, a middle-aged woman. Never once had we touched each other. Later he deposited a gift of soggy grass where I had been sitting as my reward for a job well done. Even more peculiarly his owner passed on a message for me from Joseph: 'I would not be on my own, soon I would find a new partner!'

Following the piece of luck at the sacred well, the friends predicted in Cancun magically materialised. The Pyramid of the Sun stands sixty metres high and boasts a monumental staircase climbing the five levels. As we approached, Apu focused on three people sat at the base and walked towards them. A Mexican priestess, Q'ero shaman and his travelling companion all greeted us as we arrived at the bottom of the Temple of the Sun. After a brief exchange of words, we zigzagged up the pyramid's steps to the giddy heights, surrounded by (real) ants, butterflies, eagles and dogs. Prayers were offered and the energies drawn down. On descending together we walked the avenue of the dead towards the Temple of the Moon where an invitation was extended to meet the priestess's master at Tula several days later.

On reaching the northern part of the city and high up on the Moon Temple, along with our new friends Apu laid down flat with his hands touching the ground, connecting with the energies. For a long time I sat watching. Did he tune into the great city's heyday, navigating the streets and districts, walking the north-south highway to the Great Complex which housed the market? Perhaps he felt the life of the inhabitants before this site became a great urban centre, instead an agricultural economy, somewhere around 100 BC? Or maybe the energies he felt were closer to its demise in 700 AD, when the city declined and was eventually abandoned. Could he pick up whether the cause was a natural disaster or merely another tribe defeating the vast local population?

It is more likely as Apu lay there that he reflected on Andean shamanism in the knowledge that the most important things in life are expressed in silence whilst music forms a bridge between this reality and the other. To live is to embody the supreme art of growing and to release the immense power of the heart. Maybe he connected to the laws of humility, intuition and well-meant intention. It does not matter what you say if your attitude says the opposite. Or reached a state of harmony, ready for anything and sensing all is possible.

Above: Apu calling in the Gods

Possibly, as he lay there, he understood and accepted the transcendental reason for his journey through this world and held a strong determination not to reproduce, with his desires or actions, another decrepit system. In the heat of that day he moved closer to his origins, feeling his way with his heart.

We arrived at Tula, to meet the priestess's master, and entertained ourselves in their fine archaeological museum. It was filled with yellow animal figures, a huge pair of feet (the remains of a statue of a man), ceramic pots, delicate necklaces and an unusual seat comprising a figure with raised knees. We first saw the master, seated in his feather hat, on our walk down to the pyramid. His stall looked like any other, but something attracted us to him. He sat patiently in a waistcoat and white shirt adorned with a multi-coloured hem. Around his neck were a number of beads, shrunken heads, long bone objects and a whistle. In his left hand he held a staff made of holy wood.

As we walked on, we saw the flat-topped pyramid adorned with huge Easter Island-like figures and reliefs carved into its sides, and got a sense of the city as it had once been — a city of plazas, pyramids and palaces with vast complexes of artificial terraces, canals, drainage systems, streets, boulevards and bridges spanning the Tula river. Tula was populated for more than four centuries and was one of Mexico's most important cities. Home to tens of thousands of inhabitants, it covered an area of over 16 square kilometres. Serpents adorned the entrance, and the sky was a raw blue. Later we would meet the warriors with breastplates resembling butterflies, fine feathered helmets, mirrors set in turquoise mosaics and knives.

Up on the temple roof, which in pre-Hispanic times was held up by the 'Atalantes' (human figures representing Toltec warriors) we met Hetsua, an important past life acquaintance of Apu's. He just seemed to appear, dressed in white with a deer motif on his poncho, at this solitary place on top of the world. He was as Mayan-looking as Apu was Indian. Hetsua carried a copy of the Mayan Calendar, a script for enlightenment, which he avidly explained to Apu as we sat high up on the top steps overlooking a vast grassy plaza[35]. He was keen to read Apu's personality traits based on the Mayan Calendar divination system.

Soon, others dressed in white joined us in preparation for the Eagle Meets the Condor ceremony. Then, led by the master in a feathered hat and the priestess who wore ceremonial yellow and had long black plaits, the ceremonial group and the Q'ero shaman appeared in a waft of smoke. They bowed to the pyramid temple and as one moved down onto the flat land. They then formed a circle to make offerings of fruit, precious rocks and jewels for an important ceremony joining the energies of the North and South Americas, the Eagle and the Condor as legend predicts.[36] After ceremonial speeches and personal introductions, the offerings were buried to the eerie sounds of a goat's-foot rattle and an instrument made from a gigantic shell called a *Pututu*.

The group were then led back to the pyramid, walking around the circumference to pay homage. Finally Apu and I joined the master in his hut, coming away with an ancient bone necklace and two feathers for use in healings.

Several days later, at the invitation of Hetsua, we headed for Mexico's central energetic point, Popocatelpetl, a volcano which last erupted in December 2013, to undertake the final seventh *ch'ama* ceremony. Our driver Daniel, a UFO expert

Above: Invoking the Gods with smoke and prayer

dressed in a colourful headband, talked of objects photographed in this region that distinctly resembled flying saucers. A characteristic of an energetic site is the number of stories about UFO sightings and extra-terrestrial visitors. Apu said that close to the energetic point in Lake Titicaca UFO sightings were frequent. He had witnessed a UFO himself, while conducting a ceremony with a Spanish group. Andean wisdom explains these sightings as ongoing communications between those living in the etheric cities and other beings of the cosmos. Many of the visitors are thought to be inhabitants of the Pleiades.[37]

We received gifts of turquoise necklaces and remembered the excitement of arriving in Coscomatepec, Qosqo's namesake here in Mexico. With the wispy clouds and sun above us and the pyramidal mountain looming in the distance, we sped down the highway. In the back seat we held bun-sized rocks carved with ancient, alien looking peoples with overly large heads, foot-high sculptures of the same and saucer-shaped rocks engraved from top to bottom with symbols, circles, triangles and spirals.

We climbed up through the lowlands past a yellow-spired church with eagles flying overhead and then onto a rocky road to the top. Long moments were spent digging our vehicle out of the rocky terrain, and after silent prayers for help from above, a truckload of men and women delighted in stopping to join us. Eventually, leaving the vehicle and walking the last distance with armfuls of fruit and aromatic flowers, we reached the ceremonial site.

First, Apu 'felt' the sacred spot on the river near a ford where the shallow waters ran over the road. Then he built a sacred space in a circle of small rocks. A feather was placed to mark the centre and a fire lit to draw in the energies. Dressed in various ceremonial garb including snakeskin, Mexican black ponchos and hats, the group was invited to offer up its flowers and fruit. Apu knelt, hands held high in the billowing smoke, beseeching the energies to come to us. By the close, a vision of rose blossom surrounded us all.

It was at the very end that our sign occurred. It came after our private offering, our hands held around the circle, when as a token of reciprocity Apu gave Hetsua the sun disc from around his neck. A Mexican shaman knelt in front of Apu, hands spread upwards thanking the Gods. In that moment North met South and the masculine and feminine energies were united. It was then that the sky opened and a deluge of hailstones covered the ground. The five of us returned triumphant but damp, cold and tired, having achieved our aim. For Apu and I, our *ch'ama* pilgrimage ended as it had begun, up a sacred mountain near Mendoza.

Our last days were spent in Mexico City at the witches' market – down crowded alleys crammed with one-man stalls brimming with snake skins, shrunken human skulls and phallic lovers' dolls. After a fabulous breakfast of Chinese buffet, a foreign landscape assaulted my Western senses: walking sticks with skulls carved into their knobs, bags of magical herbs and spices, antlers strung from ceilings, beads and candles, dressed skeletons, hundreds of small colourful boxes lining the walls, snake rattles and long strings of garlic. Apu was delighted, negotiating prices for beaded ceremonial bags and crystal skulls to make into power objects and sell to his clients. The air was heady with herbs, flowers and made-up potions.

Navigating the crowded streets even with the experienced help of our two Mexican friends – both shamans and masters in their own right – was an exhausting and slightly unhinging experience. Not helped by the knowledge that the next day I faced the end of my *ch'ama* pilgrimage and a long-haul flight back to the UK.

This page: And then hailstones fell from a clear sky and covered the ground

Postscript

Maria, a witch, was beginning my life review. It was a dusty environment, heavy with incense. She saw I was starting out on an emotional journey and had to decide which route to take:

See how the seven of swords lies in the Outcome position? Any new direction will be under the radar at first — you won't disclose it to anyone. Ultimately, though, the ending will be good. See the Empress card, she is the symbol for the feminine — you will have abundance and work with nature. You will reap what you sow. Now, lay your spread. Do you see that it tells an evolving story around the crumbling of an old situation if you have the courage to walk away and start something new?

My pilgrimage was completed nearly four years after this Tarot reading in Glastonbury. While it was very much my own journey, it seemed in collaboration with something bigger than myself.

Apu doesn't consider it mere coincidence that he was born when and where he was. A 'feminine' priest, he talks with *Pachamama* and receives and transmits her energies. During our time together, as I witnessed him give healings to all who asked and talk to other shamans, it became apparent he was the high level priest predicted in Don Basilio's reading. He 'adds his little grain of sand' — that is, makes his own small contribution to change this world by altering the consciousness of humans, working together with the energies of this new time. On an individual level, Apu is keen for us all to understand — in the age of Aquarius — the importance of awakening and preparing for a good death. 'Women have to prepare, and men must learn to work with their feminine energy'.

Apu consistently worked with me in an experiential way, by example not theory. His teachings are sensory-based, a matter of feelings and intuition rather than over-sentimentality or control. His words on my first trip to Peru, 'Where is love in your life?' are still with me. He challenged my pre-conceptions, absorbed and changed my energies and at times acted out my worst fears. Through his teaching, old relationships dissolved from my mind and from the very cells of my being, though a fondness and memories of good shared times remained.

So what did I learn? The first *ch'ama* taught me to release the stagnant energy and fear around long forgotten dramas. This was the start of my return to the 'Jenny' I was born to be, not the one I thought I was. The second *ch'ama* taught me to wake up, and not simply hold onto expected outcomes; rather, to trust more and discover that love should have a sweet after-taste. The third *ch'ama* taught me that the cosmos mirrors our inner dilemmas. I was encouraged to contact the shaman within and resolve old family issues. The fourth *ch'ama* showed me how to move perceptions from my mind into my body and in so doing engage fully in the moment. By detaching from subjective perception, the truth or symbolic meaning of each situation becomes clearer.

The fifth *ch'ama* taught me to be anchored in this world – in my own life and on my own path. I realised we each have our own form of expression with its unique frequency and energetic effect – the young Spanish lovers and stray dog at *Fin del Mundo* not to mention Mother Earth with her animals, birds, fish, creepy crawlies, plants, minerals, elementals and astral beings, the planets and cosmos. The sixth *ch'ama* taught me to weave my spirit into everything I do and everyone I meet. I understood that each illness and body organ has its own frequency and vibrational pattern. My ancestors became a valued part of me. In the seventh *ch'ama* I learnt to recognise the power of love, kindness and being of service, and to channel only the highest energies – the Andean *Karpays*, rites and initiations and the great masters and goddesses. Finally I understood that good things will happen when my energy is right.

My work has changed. I am better able to recognise people's tricks and blockages now. On a recent work trip to Italy, instead of becoming frustrated with my colleague's effort to read directions, I passively followed her. We walked up hill and down, in the searing morning heat. Eventually, after around an hour's walking and multiple phone-calls to our hosts, she simply gave up. 'Just up here,' I suggested and there we were. Why hadn't I intervened earlier, you might wonder? Maybe listening carefully and finding the way was her lesson not mine.

It was after the pilgrimage was completed that I first felt the desire to record and share my experiences. At five or six in the morning, the urge to put pen to paper became increasingly strong. Day by day, I relived my experiences and recapitulated the lessons. Since coming into greater harmony with the forces of nature – the hummingbirds, the hailstorm, birds circling overhead – I walk in the orchard and notice each plant's signature; its smell, its leaves, its roots, and consider its possible healing purpose. Sometimes a white feather floats down to me or is waiting on my doorstep. These signs and symbols inform my day. I interpret the messages and act accordingly in my life.

At that time those who loved me might still have described me as perhaps a little eccentric and my own woman. But I was different in both subtle and more obvious ways. Maybe increasingly authentic, happier in my own shoes, in possession of my life story and the issues I came in with. I had let go of the past and increasingly lived in the here and now. More present to others and myself. My intuition had returned. I was open to love and happy most of the time. I listened more intently and was increasingly patient, feeling the energies allowing things to come to me. I added toning, chants and rattles to my healings and passed on the information the spirits gave me. I wanted to be of service.

In June 2015, I returned to Lake Titicaca to process and consolidate the lessons of the second and third *ch'amas*. Apu and Don José asked me to join their annual Solstice ceremony and celebrate the sun coming up over the lake. I was introduced to the crowd as a white witch from the UK, and invited to talk on Puno TV about the Earth festivals we celebrate in the UK. Travelling from Puno to Qosqo, stopping again at Andahuaylillas and the church of San Pedro, my dad came to me again. This time he told me the amount of money I should give to the healing centre.

In September 2015, Apu bought a plot of land a fifteen-minute drive from Puno, in the village of Ichu-fondo close to the ancient Piramide de Inca Tunuhuiri. That same month I transferred the exact amount of money my dad had disclosed. I have donated my library of shamanic books to the healing centre. Apu says people will read them and ask him (a shaman) and I (a witch) if we can help them further.

At my sister Gilly's 60th birthday party in October, all my family gathered. People from Canada, Singapore, Sussex, Leeds and London came to Somerset - among them a Buddhist Monk, a born-again Christian, a First Nations Cree man and a leading Mindfulness practitioner. There were priests, teachers, social workers, farmers, gardeners, mariners, healers, animal communicators, artists, writers and adventurers. As Apu might say, the energies were good.

My brother-in-law Gunnar asked about Apu and was delighted to discover he had contacted other worlds to help with his knee. 'The surgeon considered it one of the most successful operations he had undertaken! Can Apu help with the next operation, as well?' Then he asked me if I knew why Lake Titicaca was famous? 'In 1970, Thor Heyerdahl, a Norwegian adventurer, sailed a boat built of papyrus across the Atlantic from Morocco. Named *Ra II*, it was built in Lake Titicaca. The trip was important, as it demonstrated mariners in the past could have dealt with trans-Atlantic voyages. Just like yours.'

Over the Winter months I learned to manage my instinctual, survival responses and mastered the fear, locked into my legs for fifty-three years. With this came an experience of joy as I no longer became overwhelmed by the small things. On 22nd

December, the day of the winter solstice, I honoured *Pachamama* at Stonehenge in the UK. I booked a holiday without knowing where I was going, just knowing that I was going to be away. Two *despacho* offerings and presents for Apu went with me. I dreamed of flying like a condor.

In mid-January 2016 I returned to Nazca and stayed with Natalia and Remy in their delightful *El Jardin* bed and breakfast. Here I revisited the Cahuachi Pyramid and sat under the 800-year-old Huarango or Algarrobo tree, got hot in the energy fields of Orcona, received a Reiki treatment from a man named Alexandro to mend the hole in my solar plexus *chakra* (and with it my over-generosity) and let the Chetzu dogs lick my feet and toes whilst I ate. I learned that Nazca is responsible for the tilt of the Earth and the first two stones in the centre of Stonehenge for the Milky Way and north and south Galactic poles.

In Arequipa I met Apu. He just appeared in front of me on the pavement outside an ATM. It was one o'clock and two hours before I was expected. We hadn't agreed a place to meet. 'Hello Jenny,' he said. I asked how he had found me and he replied, 'I am a shaman. I listen to my heart.' From here I travelled alone to Chivay, the town of love, and to Colca Canyon in search of condors. The mountains were stunningly beautiful and the air clear and crisp. *En route*, I lit a candle for Dad in the church at Yanque. I imagined him able to look out at the women with their tame eagles, children dancing in traditional dress with fringed hats and the majesty of nature in this region. The condors came, and the feathers at the end of their wings looked as if they were performing a complex *Moudra*. I stood and watched them at the edge of a sheer drop, 1,200 feet above the valley floor, without wanting to jump.

I travelled on till Puno and met with Apu again. In the warren-like streets of the market a man stopped him and whispered conspiratorially in his ear. He wanted to know the meaning of a prophetic dream. 'Not good,' Apu said and later, away from the man: 'He will have problems, maybe a death in the family. I need to see him properly, away from his work, to interpret the dream in a way he can understand.' We met with Don José and I gave him Jorge the gorilla for his collection. In a few weeks he would conduct interviews on the Candelaria festival for *Patchamama* radio. Later Apu gave a coca leaf reading and refused to make a love spell for a woman to capture her wayward boyfriend. 'There are no children involved,' he told her.

We stopped on our way out of town to diagnose a case of missing lodgers. Apu said, 'They won't return – the bed they have left is worth only 50 Peruvian sols and they owe 150.' Black smoke billowed into the skies as we passed south of the lake. 'They are asking for rain,' Apu explained, 'but on 1st August – *Pachamama* Day – I looked into the ashes and said it would be a bad year for agriculture. There is a special ceremony for making rain but *Pachamama* says no. It is not respectful to force her.' As we travelled onwards to the spiritual healing centre site, I expressed a desire to go to the islands to connect with nature. 'But Jenny, you have to be able to maintain the good energies in the city, not just on the Islands where the air and people are pure.' He continued, 'I often fight with my darker, shadow side. You don't like to do this.'

On our return, Apu spontaneously and without announcement stopped at the garage of a businessman and shaman called John. As we walked in, he said, 'I want John to confirm what you are, to show whether I am right.' John was delighted to see Apu, and said he had dreamt about Apu walking in with a strange woman six months before. We sat and introductions were made. This man's eyes were mesmerising and seemed to search deep within me. I caught the words *mucho energies, big spirit, high priestess* and *not fully awake yet* along with a request for me to bless a ceremonial object with my feminine energies. I was offered one of his sacred stones and in the spirit of *Ayni* promised to send him a model of my 'unusual' car for his vast collection.

Apu asked if I would like to join him at the Minatures festival in La Paz, Bolivia and then travel on to Sun Island. Here people buy miniature representations of their wishes for the year to place on their altars – a car, a building plot, kitchen items, diplomas. There was even a stall where you could declare your intention to get married that year, pay for the hire of wedding clothes, sit through a small ceremony and receive a pretend marriage certificate to place on your altar. As we walked around the festival Apu said, 'You are sleepwalking,' but I bought a beautiful Frida Kahlo hairbrush and was happy. Later we ambled through the cobbled streets, climbed the steep valley where houses rose vertically and ate at a quaint restaurant carefully decorated with scores of pictures, clocks, crystal chandeliers and metal knickknacks (guns, padlocks and gate grills). The next morning, Apu just upped and left. He returned to Puno angry and in a hurry, saying he no longer liked this experience.

On 25th January, the day Mercury ceased its backward movement in the sky, I understood it was time for me to walk alone, but for days it felt as if I had tight leather leggings around my calves. I visited Sun Island where 1,500 years ago around 9,000 people from Tiwanaku, survivors of drought, earthquake and crop failure, arrived with the remnants of their ancient civilisation. I chatted to a fellow visitor, Wolfgang, about his Buddhist philosophy and got historical and geographic details from Cesar, '*el mejor guia del mundo.*' Together we walked the length of the island, watched the sun set, visited the sun temple, had a beautiful ceremony with an Amauta shaman and ate pizza, whilst three young girls sang to us high up in the hills under an ink black, starry sky. At night the family dog lay outside my room. They were memorable days.

From Sun Island the people set out to establish the Incan empire, eventually planting the golden staff in Qosqo. Like them I headed to the Puma city. Going through the town of Andahuaylillas past the church of San Pedro, my father's namesake, the hills had a pink and green glow and emanated a sense of love. It wafted from them as a thin, velvety mist which was surreal and inviting. It nurtured me. There was no message from my father this time.

Lying in bed that night, streams of words and sentences seemed to appear and then float away and leave me. I was hot and feverish. At times I had conversations with Apu - 'Meet me at one o'clock in the cathedral square tomorrow for lunch.' My mouth was dry whilst my lips seemed covered in spume. It was if I were disgorging a dictionary, a book or a project plan. By daybreak I had let go of miles and miles of words, thoughts, decisions and conversations. I felt shocked and disorientated as if something were different and my head had run a half-marathon.

On 1st February I revisited the sacred site of *Sacsayhuaman* and paid a guide. She fascinated me by saying stargazers used to look into the sacred waters to view a reflection of the skies. We walked in stooped fashion through the six-metre cleansing tunnel followed by a yellow dog and numerous children, and sat on a grassy hill whilst a local shaman explained about the *chakana* or Andean Cross. Hair was very important in the Incan culture. Each follicle represented one of an infinite number of *chakras*. That evening I took the bus to Lima and onwards deep into the jungle. I travelled for forty hours.

At the refuge in Pucallpa, with the kind help of Stefania (a maestro), Henarte (a shaman) and Ta ti (an angelic helper) as well as a cleansing diet and plant medicine, I unravelled deep life dramas and found the lessons within. It was difficult and painful. I learned there were important but unresolved issues around my birth, childhood illness and heart which affected my relationships and ability to feel and trust and drove me to long periods of soporific movement in cars, buses, trains and boats and to hoarding belongings, money and food.

Ta ti said, 'Jenny, I *saw you* last night, wearing a crown dressed with red roses.' I recalled my 'here and now' ceremony and Apu's question, 'What did you feel?' Vivid in my mind was the vision of a skeleton after which came love. With help I contacted my internal shaman, formed a connection with nature and self and touched the divine.

'Our children have learned that life is a game and, if you play it, you will discover that humour is the only serious matter in life... They know that animals talk, that the trees and the river offer advice, that the mountain provides shelter and that, when a good man turns into a condor, he takes flight.'

The Gate of Paradise, Secrets of Andean Shamanism.

A note on ch'amas and chakras

The human body has seven identifiable energy centres or vortices of swirling energy known as *chakras*. This system circulates energy through the body primarily via the spinal column. Each *chakra* is situated near an endocrine gland responsible for regulating hormones in the body. A further set of *chakras* is said to be located above the crown of the head. The existence of these energy centres has been recognised by shamans, yogis, saints, sages and monks for millenia. The Yogic *Chakra* system is said to be 4,000 to 5,000 years old. The body's *chakras* can be found in the following places:

Root chakra	the perineum
Sacral chakra	3 inches below the navel
Solar plexus chakra	the upper abdomen
Heart chakra	the centre of the chest
Throat chakra	the throat
Third eye chakra	between the eyes
Crown chakra	above the head

The most commonly accepted senses, glands, activities and body parts associated with each *chakra* are:

Chakra	Sense	Gland	Activity	Body Parts
Root	Smell	Supra-renal	Fight or flight	Spinal column, bones, teeth, nails, anus, rectum, colon, blood, and the building of cells
Sacral	Taste	Prostate, ovaries, testicles	Disposal of body's rubbish	Pelvic girdle, kidneys, bladder and all liquids, such as blood, lymph, gastric juice, sperm and regulation of the female cycle
Solar Plexus	Sight	Pancreas	Metabolism	Lower back, abdomen, digestive system, stomach, liver, spleen, gallbladder, autonomic nervous system
Heart	Feeling	Thymus	Immune system	Heart, upper back, thorax and thoracic cavity, lower lungs, the blood and circulatory system and the skin
Throat	Hearing	Thyroid	Energy production	Neck, throat, jaw, ears, voice, trachea, bronchial tubes, upper lungs, oesophagus and arms
Third eye	Clairvoyance	Pineal	Regulating body clock, sleep and libido	Face, eyes, ears, nose, sinuses, cerebellum, and central nervous system
Crown	Clairsentience	Pituitary	Hormones	Cerebrum

Just as *Kundalini*[38] energy weaves itself up the spine from the root to the crown *chakras*, so energy rotates throughout the planet. The Earth's energy centres or vortices govern her health. Like the human *chakras*, each energy centre has its own unique bandwidth of energy. It is thought that the Earth's *chakras* can shift locations based on planetary cycles.

Europe, Asia and Australasia house the masculine *chakras* of the Earth. Their vertical column is in the Himalayas, while the phallus of the masculine part is Mount Everest, in Tibet. The South Americans have a similar concept to *chakras*, which are known as *ch'amas*. *Ch'amas* [39] are believed to be an integral part of *Pachamama* (Mother Earth)'s body, and run along her vertebral column, the *Cordillera de los Andes* or Andes mountains.

The *ch'amas* are all located in South, Central and North America, countries which are considered to be in the feminine[40] part of *Pachamama* (the Earth). Each *ch'ama* is associated with a different energy, an etheric city and seven connections. There is a primary energetic point, and then six further points that serve as part of the network – below, above, to the right, left, front and back. These are in neighbouring countries such as Chile, Uruguay, Brazil, Paraguay, Bolivia, Ecuador and Guatemala.

The most commonly accepted locations of the Earth's masculine and feminine *chakra / ch'ama* system are:

Masculine system	Feminine system	Chakra or Ch'ama	Significance
Mount Shasta, California	Aconcagua, Argentina	Root	Where the universal life force gathers
Lake Titicaca, Peru/Bolivia	Lake Titicaca, Peru/Bolivia	Sacral	Where primal energy births itself
Uluru or Ayers Rock, Australia	Qosqo or Cusco, Peru	Solar plexus	Where a creation legend will one day be realised
Glastonbury and Shaftesbury, England	Chavin de Huantar, Peru	Heart	Where we will open our hearts to heal the Earth
The Great Pyramids near Mount Sinai and Mount of Olives in Jerusalem	Mocoa, Putumayo, Colombia	Throat	Where the cries of the mother / the voice of the planet call for help
Roving *chakra*, Western Europe	Chichen Itza, Yucatan	Third eye	Where portals open for extra dimensional energy to enter
Mount Kallas, Himalayas, Tibet	Teotihuacan, Mexico	Crown	Where our planet connects with its spiritual destiny

There is debate about the accuracy of including Mount Shasta and Lake Titicaca in the masculine system, since they are based in both North and South America, and the Americas are home to the feminine *ch'ama* sites. After the seven feminine *ch'ama* sites in Argentina, Peru, Colombia and Mexico, it is said that there are a further five moving *ch'amas* in North America, Canada and Alaska. Brazil is also thought to have an important role in global change.

Cha'ma wisdom has been handed down through guardians of the spiritual tradition and many of its masters. It is knowledge, according to some shamans, which is still not accessible to the public, especially foreigners. Few in fact have complete understanding of this system and its potential to affect us on a global level. Today's shamans tell us that Mother Earth is sick and needs *Ayni* (reciprocity). As Apu Runa says 'She provides us with food and life. It is time to return these energies.'

The ancient American prophecies speak of a period of great transformation, and foretell a new type of human appearing on the planet — *homo luminous* — possessing wisdom and power and quite free of fear. Andean wisdom holds that we are in the period 'when day breaks before the sun comes up and feminine energy takes full effect on planet Earth.' It is anticipated that *homo luminous* will be with us by 2060. The anthropologist Dr Hank Wesselman talks of a 26,000 cycle of separation coming to an end. Whilst in the Andean tradition it is believed that every 500 years the Earth's energies alter from masculine to feminine. What we do know is that in this new time, after the beginning of the Age of Aquarius, the feminine era has well and truly begun. [41]

A note on condors

The Condor is the perfect image of Andean shamanism: a symbol of the divine feminine, it is a sacred bird that shows us where to go and a representation of the visionary journey. As such the Condor is of great interest and importance. In particular, the following facts have relevance:

New World Condors are thought to be descended from storks. In the West, storks are associated with new birth, carrying babies to their parents carefully wrapped in a sling.

Condors are scavengers and nourish themselves on carrion. The potency of their gastric juices neutralizes the toxins present and destroys certain viruses. Most importantly, condors perform a service to the ecosystem by rapidly recycling dead animals. Andean shamanic healing techniques often neutralise the heavy — *Hoocha* — energy of people, animals, birds, insects and Mother Earth (stones, trees and plants) by consuming it and returning it to *Pachamama* through the energetic navel — *Qosqo* — of the priest or *Paqo*.

Most vultures have no syrinx (vocal organs) and can only hiss, grunt or sneeze. A tenet underlying Andean philosophy is that often the important things in life are expressed in silence.

Vultures have a complex breathing apparatus and a respiratory system about three times that of a mammal of corresponding size. After the Spanish conquest of the Inca Empire, 1532 – 1572, the last bastion of Andean shamanism was high up in the mountains amongst the Q'ero peoples. They adapted their lungs to live comfortably at altitude.

At breeding time, condors prepare an assemblage of twigs and grass on the ground or a rocky shelf. Andean shamanism is, simply expressed, a way to harmonise with Mother Earth. It is a philosophy which enables us to be natural and spontaneous.

Condors are one of the most undervalued and misunderstood of birds. The Shaman or spiritual journeyman is humble and embodies the shamanic attitude. He does not seek to be valued or understood.

Condors have remarkable acuity of vision. Likewise the Shaman journeys into other worlds to gather information and conduct healings. He sees that, in this new era, *'Everything that was known as truth proves to be false and what was known as superstition turns out to be truth.'* [42]

Condors are not territorial and keep watch for companions. Similarly, on what is known as the feminine path (or path of beauty) people work from the heart, are not acquisitive and look after their loved ones and community.

Condors flap their wings as little as possible but cover hundreds of miles using air currents. They soar above Earthly difficulties and do not fear them.

We are all condors.

A note on shamanic healing

Shamanic healings work on the energies in the body to resolve old traumas and emotional blockages. They aim to return a person to the purity of their original birth state. Shamans believe each person is a microcosm of the universe and a reflection of their previous thoughts, words and deeds. Any kind of spiritual work is designed to help the subject change and move to the next level. There follow some of the terms most commonly associated with shamanic healing;

Ceremonies: Florida and Kananga water are used in various rituals including spiritual cleansing and appeasing the spirits of the dead. Flowers are commonly used as an offering – typically red and white representing the feminine and masculine principles. Andean priests often make a *despacho*, whose different elements represent family, joy, sweetness etc.

Chakra diagnosis: This is an energetic technique which pinpoints where energy is blocked. Dr Brenda Davis and Dr Alberto Villoldo have explained how the *chakra*s in the body relate to different ages in our development. For example, if someone experiences trauma at the age of two, their symptoms are likely to correspond with the root *chakra*.

Chakra principles, ages, colours, sounds, gemstones and flower essences used in different shamanic healings:

Chakra or Ch'ama	Fundamental Principle	Ages	Colour	Sound	Gemstone	Flower Essence
Root	Physical will	0 - 7 49 - 56	Red	Mmm	Ruby	Hibiscus, Aloe, Vera, Angelica
Sacral	Creative reproduction of being	7 - 14 56 - 63	Orange	Ooo	Carnelian	Poppy, Iris, Fuchsia
Solar Plexus	Shaping of things	14 - 21 63 - 70	Yellow	Orr	Citrin	Sunflower, Buttercup, Sweet Pea
Heart	Devotion, self-abandonment	21 - 28 70 - 77	Green	Ahh	Rose quartz	Rose, Apple Blossom, Lavender
Throat	Resonance of being	28 - 35 77 - 85	Blue	Ehh	Turquoise	Lilac, Violet, Borage
Third Eye	Knowledge of being	35 - 42 85 - 92	Violet	Eee	Lapis	Water Lily, Passion Flower, Pansy
Crown	Purest being	42 - 49 92 - 99	White	High Ooo, Zzz	Amethyst	Lotus, Bells of Ireland, Orchid

Cleansings: *Limpia* is a cleansing of the soul and body. The aim is to remove unhelpful energies, restore the subject to power and change their 'luck' so they are blessed with greater health and stability. Shamans use tobacco or flowers, spray-perfumed *agua florida*, the smoke of *palo santo* and magical herbs. One intriguing method uses an egg – the universal symbol of the soul – to divine areas of unbalanced energy within the patient's body and rebalance them.

Demonstration and practical methods: The spirits at Aconcagua dictated Apu should teach through demonstration and practical methods and that the teachings should be simple and easy to understand. At times, his world reflected mine.

Divination: A process for gaining insight into a question or situation by way of an occult tool, using a standardized process or ritual. Varieties of divination include coca leaf, bean, ashes in the fire, rune and tarot readings.

Dreams: Dreams are considered to be our unconscious 'talking' in our night world. Dream conversations can put old issues to rest and enable people to move on.

Embodiment: The world around us reflects the lessons we need to learn. This can be as simple as opening a book at random and reading the message that is needed, or as complex as re-enacting events with others.

Energies: The practitioner eats heavy energy or *hoocha* through their energetic navel or *qosqo*. Priests place their *mesa*, or hands, on the navel and pray whilst the practitioner concentrates on giving up their heavy energies. These energies are then given back to Mother Earth who is said to enjoy a good meal.

Gifts: Gifts received on my pilgrimage included two white feathers at Spirit Valley, two small rocks representing masculine and feminine at Lake Titicaca, a brown feather for healing work (from the master at Tula) a cosmic rock (from the shaman and businessman in Puno) and a crown for protection in the Peruvian jungle.

Initiations: Of the vast array of initiations in the Andean shamanic tradition, the *Flight of the Condor* encourages connection with your divine self, while *Living in the Here and Now* encourages living in the moment.

Journeying: Shamans make small localised changes in the flow of reality, causing ordinary reality to jump. To do this they use a universal map containing upper, lower and middle worlds. The middle world exists on both a spiritual and physical reality whereas the upper and lower worlds only exist in a spiritual reality. The spirits with whom shamans work are all-knowing but not all-powerful, requiring the shaman to work in partnership with them.

Offerings: Offerings are made to *Pachamama* to thank her for everything she gives to us. Often they are in the form of flowers and alcohol. These offerings may take place at ceremonies where they heighten the energies already present.

Pachamama: Every material object, place, human, animal and plant has a spirit or energetic aspect. The seven feminine *ch'amas* Aconcagua, Lake Titicaca, Qosqo, Chavin de Huantar, Mocoa, Chichen Itza and Teotihuacan act as powerful, healing energy vortexes. Qosqo cathedral is reported to be an energetic opening to the superior world or world of refined energies. In the UK, Glastonbury Tor (and surrounding high ground) and Silbury Hill (and Waden Hill) are said to be representations of the Earth Mother, with the landscape embodying the head and body of a pregnant woman. Stonehenge, on the other hand, is reported to be a crown *chakra* and time portal, where the circular earthworks represent the head.

Plant medicines: Plant spirits are one of the shaman's major allies in the task of healing, seeing, dreaming and empowering. These plants are the messengers of divinity, harmony, beauty and poetry for the soul. It is said that the 'spirits' of *Ayahuasca* give access to an intrinsic part of the vast cosmic mind (or field of consciousness) allowing communion in the true sense of the word. Chemically, this plant allows us to retrieve previously blocked memories. Cactus ceremonies are traditionally held to cure illness, read the future, overcome sorcery, rekindle enthusiasm for life and enable one to experience the world as divine. They can put us in a telepathic state so we may transmit thoughts and feelings across time and space, filling us with love, light and laughter. *Shuauaco*, prescribed in Pucallpa, gives energy and strength whilst *Chuwase* is an anti-inflammatory which balances the hormones and is good for the stomach and intestines.

Past life regression: A shamanic technique which helps to access other lifetimes. It may take many lifetimes to release the ties.

Power animals: Helping spirits which reside in all of us, adding to our power and protecting us from illness. Each animal has different qualities: for example, a falcon spirit lends attributes such as perspective, attention and commitment once a choice is made.

Re-connecting with birth energies: The hill and river closest to your birth place are of significance and should be honoured.

Re-connecting with ancestral energies: Immediate family are important in terms of inherited traits, traumas, experiences and illnesses.

Rites: Energetic 'transmissions' designed to upgrade a person's luminous energy field and heal the karmic and genetic programmes of the past. Personal and ancestral memories, trauma and past life wounds are stored like computer programs ready to be activated, and compel us towards certain behaviours which are employed time and again even if they do not serve us.

Rituals: All shamanic traditions observe rituals around dying. One entails burning a prayer bundle made of paper, fabric or even pieces of clothing which represents the dying person's life. As the bundle burns, the soul is transformed and cleansed for the next part of its journey. Eastern medicine, particularly in Chinese and Tibetan culture, has an energy-based approach to death. The various stages of dying and the survival of spiritual consciousness are all catalogued. Central to the Tibetan concept is the *Bardos* (afterlife). A similar understanding can be found in the Andean tradition.

Runes: used by the early Anglo-Saxons as an alphabet. Each rune has a sound related to the phonetics of its name and holds a meaning connected to the sacred mysteries of the cosmos.

Shape shifting: Shamans are reported to be able to shift into, and travel in, different forms. Apu claims he shape shifted into a beautiful red and orange butterfly which visited me one day.

Soul contract: An agreement we have consciously or unconsciously made that may no longer be appropriate.

Soul retrieval: An ancient shamanic tradition for healing emotional and physical illness.

Trauma work: Shamanic practices encourage the release of locked-in trauma. This requires the practitioner to have an understanding of the fight or flight response – and the implications when this response is not physically-activated, at the time of the event, and the trauma stored in the body.

For more information about shamanic practice the reader is directed to: *Shaman, Healer, Sage. How to heal yourself and others with the energy medicine of the americas.*

Alberto Villoldo, Ph.D. Bantam Books.

Endnotes

Lead Up

1. Rupert Sheldrake talks of our habits creating morphogenetic fields in a 'higher' dimension. This information wraps itself around our existing structures and makes up our personal operating system. Quantum theory supports the idea that the world is as we dream it.

Dr Bruce Lipton says we spend the first seven years of our life in a hypnotic trance, downloading programmes from the environment around us, only some of which result in helpful behaviours. These programmes guide our lives. The construction and destruction of these programmes depends upon vibration. A Shaman can influence our vibration or the pattern of the programmes which exist.

2. Telepathy can be received in four primary ways by a person - clairvoyance (seeing visual images) claircognizance (a feeling or inner knowing) clairsentience (feeling on an empathetic level) and more rarely clairaudience (hearing a voice).

3. The Munai Ki rites are a series of energetic transmissions designed to upgrade our luminous energy field and heal the karmic and genetic programs of the past. They are associated with the work of Dr Alberto Villoldo. Currently, there are thirteen Munai Ki rites, with the recent addition of the rite of the womb.

4. It is a great honour to receive this rite.

5. The Emotional Freedom Technique (EFT) combines Chinese acupressure and modern psychology to stimulate the body's energy meridian points with the fingertips — literally tapping into the body's energy and healing power.

6. Florida water is a revitalizing scent, while Kananga water is a cologne with a base scent of Ylang Ylang. Both are used in various rituals including spiritual cleansing and appeasing the spirits of the dead.

7. An etheric city is a city that exists in a parallel dimension.

Ch'ama One

8. See 'Journeying' in A Note on Shamanic Healing

9. Hoocha means heavy energy in Qechua. In the Incan tradition, energy (kausay) is heavy when it stagnates or is blocked. Sami refers to energy that flows or becomes light. As humans have free will, it is said they can both block and allow energy flow.

10. Giants often represent one's animal or instinctual side in Norse or Saxon mythology.

Ch'ama Two

11. Dr David Hamilton says mood is contagious — either happy or depressed. Each person affects the mental health of people in their social network by three degrees of separation.

12. Horses often mirror suppressed emotions. They are uncomfortable with incongruence, such as a human putting on a happy face whilst his blood pressure rises and muscles tense.

13. A meridian is an energy channel that runs through the body and is used in healing therapies including acupuncture.

14. Blackbirds can symbolise a need to let go of inhibitions and sing to connect with the nature spirits. A gateway of the non-ordinary world beckoning one to follow one's true spiritual path.

15. A term often used to denote a smell like bad eggs and thought to mean 'God of the Storm.'

Ch'ama Three

16. Characters in the legend of the return of fish to Lake Titicaca, see previous chapter.

17. One of the Andean initiations for becoming an adult enables the release of the spiritual impurities connected to one's parents since conception, replaced by a connection with Mother Earth.

18. R.D. Laing, an eminent psychiatrist and empath, describes a female patient who rocked back and forth and refused to wear any clothes. When he took off his own clothing and sat next to her rocking at the same tempo, she asked who he was and a dialogue was begun. 'Shall we put some clothes on and go and have dinner together?' he asked. This was the start of her re-joining society.

Ch'ama Four

19. Angaangaq Angakkorsuaq, a Shaman from Greenland, has spoken about the possibility of changing a person for the better by blowing his breath into them. Energetic transmission in various forms, (hands on head, breath etc.) is a worldwide shamanic practice.

20. Death of the mortal body is said to be the final spiritual ascent. The 'unquiet dead' have not transcended to where they want to go, and are often dispirited/have experienced - soul loss -, or had a traumatic or sudden death. Shamans facilitate safe passage. An Aboriginal elder says the spirits show themselves in natural forms such as rocks and trees — differently to each of us, but in a form we understand.

21. People often carry memories of painful family experiences as well as particular ways of thinking and doing things. Participants in family constellation exercises exhibit an uncanny ability to 'know' about the family system and reveal core fears or symptoms. Often the trauma has occurred in a prior generation.

22. Lightning is said to represent a sudden and unexpected descent of Divine Light signifying connection with unfathomable power. It activates a spiritual rebirth in the one who experiences it and that person is touched by the god / goddess.

23. Ostriches indicate a need to let go whatever is no longer useful to us. They have links with the sensate world.

24. The San Pedro cactus, sometimes referred to as 'El Remedio,' is one of the most ancient of the magical 'teacher plants'. One of the cactus's guardian spirits is the hummingbird. See also 'Plant Medicines' entry in A Note on Shamanic Healing.

Ch'ama Five

25. Apu tells the story of a woman coming to his master for a healing. She complained of having inadequate funds when he charged her five sols. The master said this was his work and insisted she pay him as he had to feed his family. When asked by Apu why he insisted on payment, his master replied that his hands work separately. He charges with the one hand. Meanwhile, with the other he slips twenty sols into her shopping bag.

26. A road train is a big truck towing two or more trailers used in the remote areas of Australia.

27. Lemuria or Mu is the name of a hypothetical lost land usually located in the Pacific Ocean. It is said that at the peak of its civilization, the Lemurian people were both highly evolved and very spiritual.

Ch'ama Six

28. The term Ley lines has two meanings. The older refers to the ancient, straight trackways in the British landscape, while the newer refers to spiritual and mystical alignments of land forms.

29. Bruce Chatwin says the melodic contour of the songs described the nature of the land over which the ancestors' feet travelled. An expert Song-man could calculate where he was at any point along a Songline.

30. Sound healing is one way Shamans bring the vibration of the healing universe and the powers of nature into their body, opening themselves up to a deeper awareness.

31. Sacrifice was key to Mayan culture and founded on knowledge about how the soul can face the ultimate terror and rise again 'in a paradise beyond its wildest dreams.'

32. Katherine Maltwood has described a ten-mile wide circle of zodiacal figures etched into the Somerset landscape making use of natural features.

Ch'ama Seven

33. The Feathered Serpent was a prominent supernatural entity or deity, called variously Quetzalcoatl, Kukulkan, Q'uq'umatz and Tohil. It represented the duality of nature. Snakes commonly represent entities of renewal, guardians of the mysteries of birth and regeneration and the umbilical cord, joining all humans to Mother Earth.

34. Skulls, in particular crystal skulls, are reported to have strong electronic properties.

35. The Mayan calendar dates back to around 5BC and consists of a system of three interlacing calendars and almanacs. The calendar moves in cycles with the final cycle ending in December 2012.

36. An ancient prophecy — more than 2,000 years old — which relates to the two different paths that humans have taken throughout history, the path of the Eagle or Condor. These two paths have diverged at times, but it is predicted that they will potentially conjoin to become one and create a higher level of consciousness.

37. The Pleiades is a small cluster of seven stars located in the constellation of Taurus. The inhabitants, known as Pleiadians, are said to be a highly-evolved humanoid race and the next step in our evolution to gain enlightenment. They radiate a fifth-dimensional frequency of love and creativity, and have a 'Goddess Society' which worships family, children and women. Their spirituality is grounded in service to the greater good, with a collective consciousness of love, peace, and wisdom.

A Note on Ch'amas and Chakras

38. The Kundalini, is experienced physically as an electric current running along the spine and is often represented as a goddess or sleeping serpent. An awakening is said to result in enlightenment or bliss and involves moving the 'coiled' energy from the base of the spine up the central channel to the top of the head.

39. In Incan or Quechuan language, words like ch'ama are pronounced with the accent on the next to last syllable – a sounds like ah and ch is pronounced like the ch in chair.

40. Joseph Campbell links the image of the Earth or Mother Goddess to symbols of fertility and reproduction. 'The human woman gives birth just as the Earth gives birth to the plants... so woman magic and Earth magic are the same. They are related. And the personification of the energy that gives birth to forms and nourishes forms is properly female.'

The Goddess traditions are often associated with love, compassion, understanding, intuition, insight, creativity, forgiveness, magic and wisdom. They symbolize balance and healing, renewal and restoration. The Goddess may appear as Gaia or Quan Yin, as Mother Mary or the mysterious Black Madonna or Black Virgin or one of the pantheon of goddesses from ancient Egypt, Greece or Rome such as Isis or Sophia. She is present in Africa and the Middle East and as an archetype in indigenous tribes where feminine qualities, like those of a child, include being humble, innocent, trusting, loving and - most importantly - naturally happy all the time.

41. *16th – 17th August 1987 (the harmonic convergence) saw the end of the nine hells and the beginning of the thirteen heavens in the Aztec calendar, meaning the end of the suppression of the wisdom of Mesoamerica. The alignment is said to have altered the physical and psychic field of our planet, instigating a galaxy-orientated perspective.*

A Note on Condors

42. *Luis Espinoza Chamalu,* The Gate of Paradise, Secrets of Andean Shamanism. Gateway Books

As I write, there is no electricity at the healing centre site and Apu Runa needs to carry water, in a bucket, from a large muddy hole outside the walls. Work has temporarily ground to a halt with the initial funds having been spent. With further paid work from spiritual tourists building will recommence.

Apu Runa can be contacted by email on aramuraul@hotmail.com

Jenny can be contacted via www.twowhitefeathers.com

With Thanks

Big thanks to Matt Bryden for my writing tuition and his wonderful editing job.

Also to Fulvio Naselli for improving my photography skills and bringing my photographs alive, Patrick Barber for encouraging me to learn from indigenous healers at source and helping my body endure the hardship of long-haul flights and two-day bus journeys, Janet Pipes for my wonderful hats, Sarah Fry for trying every which way to teach me Spanish and Blossom Evans and Lucy Pearce for their design and publishing help and Nick Brett for the **two white feathers** website. Along with Kenneth Mortimer and Maru Hernandez for their translation into Spanish and Don Jose Morales for his invaluable cultural input to the writing style.

With special thanks to Eliana Harvey, establisher of Shamanka Traditional School of Women's Shamanism for her lifelong commitment to working with wounded and abused women.

And to fellow students Sandy Pennell for her enduring friendship and teachings, Maria Moonstar who shared her beloved South American Shamans, Tracey-Lee Scully for her editorial help with the feminine ch'amas article in the July/August 2015 issue of **Kindred Spirit**, Bernadette Shaw for her magical healings at our annual healing stand, Rosemary Taylor for her creative shamanic sound healings and my powerful release and Carol Druce author of **Stonehenge Experience** for guiding me and sharing her experiences of the Henge on the 2015 solstice.

Thank you to Leanna Milward and Shelley Rosenberg for my education in equine facilitated learning and to Livvy Adams for sharing the experience with me. Thanks to Maria Gletherow at the Wonky Broomstick in Glastonbury for my tarot lessons and education in witchcraft. Particular thanks to Stefania Pastorelli, Henarte Seijas Guerra and Ta ti for my cleansing and plant medicine retreat.

Thanks to all my family and good friends and to the people I met along the route and particularly to those of you who embodied special lessons for me.

Most of all thanks to Raul Juan Tomaylla Lezama (Apu Runa), healer and Shaman, for persevering with me and never faltering in his determination to help me feel, and in so doing, understand my life lessons. He is a very special man.

Author

Jenny has practised as a Rehabilitation Counsellor for nearly thirty years helping people who have suffered illness, injury or accident return to work. She is a published author and lectured at masters level in her field. For a number of years she worked as an Open University tutor and undertook student disability assessments in Northern Ireland.

In recent years she has worked with universities, schools, governments and private training organisations to transfer best practice in vocational rehabilitation, across Europe. The transfer materials were based on a course her company developed, which was accredited at undergraduate and postgraduate levels by the University of Derby. Each organisation set out to educate partners into their culture and rehabilitation techniques which has left her with a raft of experiences and wonderful memories of Austria, Bulgaria, Czech Republic, Estonia, Germany, Greece, Italy, Latvia, Lithuania, Poland, Romania, Slovenia, Spain and Turkey.

Jenny is a qualified shamanic practitioner and horse whisperer. In the last year she has been invited to teach on the Luminous Warrior 2nd year training course at Shamanka Traditional School of Women's Shamanism and to be a Trustee for Painted Horse, a charity involved with self-empowerment and leadership for abused women and their families.

Jenny's healing work has been informed by significant travel experiences including crossing Eastern Africa in a truck, a Mediterranean, trans-Atlantic and Caribbean yacht delivery, fifteen years living in the outback, Snowy Mountains and coastal regions of Australia and a three-week train trip through China, Mongolia, Russia and Northern Europe to Bristol in the UK. In recent years she has set out to work with and learn directly from healers from different indigenous cultures. In 2014, she initiated the journey described in this book, with Apu, through South and Central America to visit and activate the seven feminine *ch'amas* or energetic earth centres.

Jean Macmillan Chapman illustrated this book at age 84 years. She is my mum.

'A fascinating travel book taking you to many spiritually significant locations in South and Central America. The shaman, Apu, proves to be an inspirational guide explaining his Andean philosophy and heart based healing methods on route. Like 'tapping' this journey has the ability to alter your DNA and realign your experiences to manifest a different reality. An incredible adventure into the world of healing and spirituality.'

Karl Dawson. EFT Founding Master, Creator Of Matrix Reimprinting, Hay House Author.

'A beautiful book which I couldn't put down. As with the teachings at Shamanka, Jenny writes about practical ways to transform and heal our lives and that of the Earth. With simple explanations of indigenous healing methods, descriptions of sacred sites and life on the road she sets the scene for our transition into the divine feminine. Jenny's enchanting journey unfolds as she listens to the intelligence of her heart.'

Eliana Harvey. Establisher of Shamanka, traditional school of women's shamanism.

www.ingramcontent.com/pod-product-compliance
Lightning Source LLC
Chambersburg PA
CBHW042100290426
44113CB00005B/105